Edexcel Anthology of Poetry

Conflict

Edexcel's *Conflict* poetry cluster has its fair share of poems about war and writing essays about them can be a real battle.

Not to worry. This brilliant book guides you through the entire cluster — form, structure, language, themes, context... the lot. And because it's from CGP, we get straight to the point, with no needless rambling.

We've also included plenty of practice questions to test you on what you've learned, plus a whole section of advice to help you write top-grade answers. Everything you need to emerge victorious in the exams!

The Poetry Guide

CONTENTS

Contents

Published by CGP

Editors:
Marc Barnard
Tom Carney
Sean Walsh

With thanks to James Summersgill and Nicola Woodfin for the proofreading.
With thanks to Ana Pungartnik for the copyright research.

Acknowledgements:

Quote on the cover and poem 'Belfast Confetti' by Ciaran Carson. Reproduced by kind permission of the author and The Gallery Press, Loughcrew, Oldcastle, County Meath, Ireland from *Collected Poems (2008)*

HALF-CASTE copyright © 1996 by John Agard reproduced by kind permission of John Agard c/o Caroline Sheldon Literary Agency Ltd.

'Catrin' from Collected Poems by Gillian Clarke (Carcanet Press Limited, 1997)

'War Photographer' by Carole Satyamurti from *Stitching the Dark: New & Selected Poems (Bloodaxe Books, 2005)*.
Reproduced by permission of Bloodaxe Books. www.bloodaxebooks.com

'The Class Game' complete poem by Mary Casey from I WOULDN'T THANK YOU FOR A VALENTINE edited by Carol Ann Duffy (Puffin, 1992). Copyright © Carol Ann Duffy 1992. Reproduced by permission of Penguin Books Ltd.

'Poppies' by Jane Weir: Copyright Templar Poetry from *The Way I Dressed During the Revolution* (Templar, 2010)

'No Problem' by Benjamin Zephaniah from *Propa Propaganda (Bloodaxe Books, 1996)*.
Reproduced by permission of Bloodaxe Books. www.bloodaxebooks.com

'What Were They Like' by Denise Levertov from *New Selected Poems (Bloodaxe Books, 2003)*.
Reproduced by permission of Bloodaxe Books. www.bloodaxebooks.com

Every effort has been made to locate copyright holders and obtain permission to reproduce sources. For those sources where it has been difficult to trace the copyright holder of the work, we would be grateful for information. If any copyright holder would like us to make an amendment to the acknowledgements, please notify us and we will gladly update the book at the next reprint. Thank you.

ISBN: 978 1 78908 000 1
Printed by Elanders Ltd, Newcastle upon Tyne.
Clipart from Corel®

Based on the classic CGP style created by Richard Parsons.

How to Use this Book

This book is for anyone studying the 'Conflict' cluster of the Edexcel GCSE English Literature Poetry Anthology. You'll have to answer an exam question on the poems — this book tells you what you need to know.

You need to know the poems really well

You need to know all fifteen poems in depth. Read each one carefully over and over again, and jot down your own ideas about it. This book will help you understand the poems and develop your ideas:

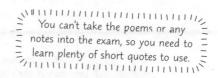
You can't take the poems or any notes into the exam, so you need to learn plenty of short quotes to use.

- Section One guides you through each poem in the cluster — read the notes on what each poem means, its main features, and the attitudes and feelings it conveys.

- Answer the questions about each poem — these will help you develop a personal response to it.

- When you feel that you know the poems well, have a go at the questions at the end of the section. They'll help you identify any gaps in your knowledge of the poems.

In the exam, you have to compare poems

1) The Poetry Anthology question will give you one poem from the 'Conflict' cluster and ask you to choose another to compare it to, usually based on a certain theme.

2) In Section Two the poems are grouped by theme, to give you some ideas of which poems you could compare in the exam and what you might say about them.

3) Have a go at the practice questions at the end of the section to check you're up to speed with the themes of each poem.

Have a look inside the front cover for a handy summary of which themes relate to which poems.

Get to grips with the main features of each poem

1) Section Three is all about form, structure and language.

2) It looks at how different poets use techniques like rhyme, rhythm and imagery to create effects — the examiners are really keen for you to write about this.

3) There are some more practice questions at the end of the section to help you test your knowledge.

First day on the job, and Tim had already got to grips with the 'self-destruct' feature of his car.

Learn how to write a cracking exam answer

1) You need to know how to write a great essay comparing two poems:

- Section Four gives you loads of advice on how to plan and write a fantastic exam answer.

- There are several extracts from sample answers to show you the right way to approach the question.

2) Once you know the theory, put it into practice:

- Section Five lets you test your skills by adding quotes or extending points to improve essay extracts. This will help you understand how to really use the poems to write a top-notch answer.

- It also gives you some sample answers to grade, which will help you to improve your own answers.

3) There's no substitute for getting some practice at writing essays:

- Use what you've learnt to answer the exam-style questions at the end of Sections One, Two and Three.

- You don't have to write a full essay for every question — making a detailed plan is still good practice.

A Poison Tree

First-person speaker personalises the poem and makes it seem more real.

This stanza is an example of antithesis. By placing two contrasting statements close to each other, Blake highlights the contrast between what happened when the speaker expressed their anger and when they didn't.

Repeating "I was angry" at the start of these lines places emphasis on anger being a key feeling in the poem.

I was angry with my friend:
I told my wrath, my wrath did end.
I was angry with my foe:
I told it not, my wrath did grow.

The speaker suggests that anger, like a plant, needs to be fed to grow. He 'feeds' his anger with his "tears".

Tries to conceal their anger, though this only helps it grow. Sibilance mimics the sound of hissing, which makes their masking of anger seem sinister.

5 And I water'd it in fears,
Night and morning with my tears;
And I sunned it with smiles,
And with soft deceitful wiles.

It's ironic that the poet uses the idea of a tree growing to represent the speaker's anger, as this usually has positive connotations.

The tree becomes more active in this stanza — "it grew" contrasts with the passive "I water'd it" on line 5. It is as if the anger is no longer under the speaker's control.

And it grew both day and night,
10 Till it bore an apple bright;
And my foe beheld it shine,
And he knew that it was mine,

Apples are symbolic of temptation and sin, as they are often associated with the forbidden fruit in the Book of Genesis.

It's not clear why the foe sneaks into the garden. The ambiguity leaves it up to the reader to decide if they think the foe went to cause mischief, or if the speaker planned to lure them there all along.

And into my garden stole
When the night had veil'd the pole:
15 In the morning glad I see
My foe outstretch'd beneath the tree.

Repetition of "And" adds a sense of urgency to the poem, as well as making it sound childlike.

The pole star was used to guide people to safety, but it's described as "veil'd", which suggests hidden danger.

The use of "glad" is ambiguous — it could be referring to the morning, or to the speaker. If referring to the speaker, these final lines give the poem a sinister climax, as the speaker looks pleased that their foe has collapsed.

Context — 'Book of Genesis'
The apple in the poem could be an allusion to the story of Adam and Eve. In the Bible, God forbids Adam and Eve from eating the fruit from the tree of knowledge. However, they both eat the fruit after Eve is tempted to do so by a snake. God punishes them, and all of humanity, for their sin. Although it isn't specified in the Bible, the fruit is often depicted as an apple.

POEM DICTIONARY
told — confessed
wrath — anger
foe — enemy
wiles — clever tricks that are used to manipulate people
pole — the pole star, a star often used for navigation

William Blake

'A Poison Tree' was published in 1794. It's from a volume of Blake's poetry called 'Songs of Experience', which explored the human soul, focusing on how innocence is lost and how society has been corrupted.

You've got to know what the poem's about

1) The speaker describes the <u>consequences</u> of leaving your anger to build up, rather than speaking about it.

2) Their anger is described like a poison tree, which keeps <u>growing</u> until it produces a <u>poisonous</u> apple that harms or potentially kills their enemy.

3) The poem is <u>ambiguous</u>. The speaker might be presenting a <u>cautionary tale</u> (warning the reader not to make the mistakes they made). However, in the final stanza, it can be interpreted that the speaker is glad about their enemy's possible death, which adds a <u>disturbing</u> twist to the events.

Learn about the form, structure and language

1) **FORM** — The poem has a very <u>simple</u> rhyme scheme made up of <u>rhyming couplets</u>. This creates a <u>regular beat</u> and makes it sound like a <u>nursery rhyme</u>, which emphasises that it has a moral message.

2) **STRUCTURE** — The first stanza introduces the <u>moral</u> of the poem. The following stanzas introduce and develop the <u>extended metaphor</u> of the tree as it grows. The final stanza also provides the poem's <u>climax</u>, as it's implied that the speaker's building anger has led to the foe's <u>death</u>.

3) **CONTRASTS** — The poem uses <u>contrasts</u> to emphasise a <u>moral message</u>. The speaker compares a time when they <u>spoke about</u> their anger with a time they <u>hid</u> it — this direct contrast shows what the <u>consequences</u> of repressing your emotions can be. In the second stanza, Blake contrasts "tears" with "smiles" to show that whatever the speaker did, their <u>anger</u> would grow — it was <u>out of control</u>.

4) **NATURAL LANGUAGE** — The speaker's anger is described using the <u>metaphor</u> of a poison tree, which they "sunned" and "water'd" with their emotions, causing it to <u>grow</u> naturally.

5) **REPETITION** — Many of the lines in the poem begin with "<u>And</u>". Repeating the same words at the <u>start</u> of consecutive lines or sentences is called <u>anaphora</u>. This example gives the impression that the speaker is trying to tell the story <u>quickly</u>, as well as reflecting the <u>constant</u> growth of the speaker's <u>anger</u>.

Remember the feelings and attitudes in the poem

1) **ANGER** — People can be angry with <u>friends</u> and <u>foes</u>. Describing anger through the metaphor of a <u>tree</u> shows that it is not only a <u>natural</u> emotion, but it is also an emotion that can easily grow <u>out of control</u>.

2) **DECEPTION** — Both the speaker and their foe act <u>deceivingly</u>. The speaker hides their anger with <u>insincere</u> smiles, while the foe <u>sneaks</u> into the speaker's garden.

3) **REPRESSION** — The poem suggests that negative emotions (such as anger) cause more <u>damage</u> if they're <u>ignored</u> and not spoken about.

Go a step further and give a personal response

Have a go at <u>answering</u> these <u>questions</u> to help you come up with <u>your own ideas</u> about the poem:

Q1.	Do you think the poem presents a clear moral message? Why / why not?
Q2.	Do you think the tree is an effective metaphor? Explain why.
Q3.	Why do you think the speaker's enemy sneaks into the garden?

Anger, conflict in society, effects of conflict, nature...

The feeling of anger is also present in poems such as 'Half-caste', 'The Class Game' and 'Cousin Kate'. You could also compare how nature is used in 'Exposure', 'The Prelude' and 'What Were They Like?'.

The Destruction of Sennacherib

Not referring to Sennacherib by name and using a third-person perspective creates a sense of distance.

This simile likens Sennacherib to a wolf, suggesting that he is a dangerous predator. The Israelites are likened to sheep, a symbol of innocence.

Colours show the wealth and power of the Assyrian army. Purple was a colour often worn by kings.

Simile comparing the soldiers to natural phenomena makes the army seem impressive. However, comparing them to reflections on the surface of the water implies they have no substance.

Focus on shiny surfaces suggests that the Assyrians are only superficially impressive and lack real substance.

The Assyrian came down like the wolf on the fold,
And his cohorts were gleaming in purple and gold;
And the sheen of their spears was like stars on the sea,
When the blue wave rolls nightly on deep Galilee.

Repetition helps to highlight the turning point in the narrative.

5 Like the leaves of the forest when Summer is green,
That host with their banners at sunset were seen:
Like the leaves of the forest when Autumn hath blown,
That host on the morrow lay wither'd and strown.

Comparing the change in the Assyrians' fortune to the change of the seasons makes their defeat seem natural and inevitable.

The repetition of "And" drives the narrative forward.

For the Angel of Death spread his wings on the blast,
10 And breathed in the face of the foe as he pass'd;
And the eyes of the sleepers wax'd deadly and chill,
And their hearts but once heaved, and for ever grew still!

Alliteration of 'f' mimics the sound of the breath.

Alliteration of 'h' slows down the narrative and sounds like a final exhale of breath.

And there lay the steed with his nostril all wide,
But through it there roll'd not the breath of his pride:
15 And the foam of his gasping lay white on the turf,
And cold as the spray of the rock-beating surf.

The Angel of Death is not violent as might be expected — instead, he calmly kills the soldiers.

Creates a disturbing image of the horse's death — it's a far more violent image than the description of how the soldiers die.

Contrasts with the earlier description of the army "gleaming".

And there lay the rider distorted and pale,
With the dew on his brow and the rust on his mail;
And the tents were all silent, the banners alone,
20 The lances unlifted, the trumpet unblown.

Caesurae and end-stopping create pauses which emphasise the silence of the battlefield.

The idea of 'silence' around the soldiers' deaths creates an almost peaceful image.

And the widows of Ashur are loud in their wail,
And the idols are broke in the temple of Baal;
And the might of the Gentile, unsmote by the sword,
Hath melted like snow in the glance of the Lord!

Screams from Assyrian women create a heightened sense of emotion that contrasts with the silence of the battlefield.

Idols are objects that are worshipped as a god. Worshipping these objects was considered sinful.

Here, the "Gentile" refers to Sennacherib.

Gentle nature simile shows how easily God can destroy and reinforces the calm, almost natural defeat of the Assyrians.

The poem ends by emphasising the power of God.

POEM DICTIONARY
fold — can mean both 'a flock of sheep' or 'a group with shared religious belief'
cohorts — members of a group (cohort is also an old-fashioned word for a group of soldiers)
Galilee — a region in northern Israel
host — an old-fashioned word for 'army'
Angel of Death — an angel sent by God to kill enemies of the Israelites
wax'd — an old-fashioned word for 'grew'
mail — armour made of metal rings linked together
Ashur — the capital city of the ancient Assyrian Empire
Baal — a god worshipped in the ancient Middle East, considered a 'false god' by the Israelites
Gentile — someone who isn't Jewish
unsmote — not hit

Context — 2 Kings 18-19
'The Destruction of Sennacherib' is based on a short Bible story from the Old Testament (from chapters 18 and 19 of the second Book of Kings). It's about an attempt by the Assyrian army to seize Jerusalem, the holy city of the Israelites. Assyria was a kingdom in the ancient Middle East.

Lord Byron

Lord Byron was a Romantic poet — Romanticism was an artistic movement in the 18th and 19th centuries which put emphasis on emotion and nature. 'The Destruction of Sennacherib' was published in 1815.

You've got to know what the poem's about

1) King Sennacherib's large and powerful Assyrian army prepare to attack the holy city of Jerusalem.

2) The Angel of Death is sent by God to defeat the Assyrian army. He calmly and mysteriously kills the Assyrian soldiers and their horses before they have the chance to attack Jerusalem.

3) Back in the city of Ashur, the soldiers' widows grieve and the idols in the temple are destroyed.

Learn about the form, structure and language

1) **FORM** — The poem is written in rhyming couplets — these drive the poem forward, reflecting the quick defeat of the Assyrians. The regular rhythm might also remind the reader of galloping horses.

2) **STRUCTURE** — The poem tells the story in chronological order. The first stanza describes the initial glory of the Assyrian army. However, on line 7, there's a turning point (volta) — from then on, the poem describes the Assyrians' defeat.

3) **APPEARANCES** — Much of the imagery surrounding the Assyrian army describes their surface appearance. This suggests that their strength is superficial compared to God, who is far more powerful.

4) **NATURAL IMAGERY** — The poet compares things to nature. He shows Sennacherib's violence by comparing him to a wolf, and compares the quick defeat of the Assyrians to the change of the seasons.

5) **REPETITION** — Byron uses anaphora (repeating the same words at the start of consecutive lines or sentences) to highlight the poem's turning point and drive the poem forward — it creates a sense of momentum and inevitability.

6) **SILENCE AND STILLNESS** — For a poem about war, a lot of the language that's used creates a sense of calm. This gives the poem an eerie tone, while also emphasising how God's power is effortless compared to the big displays of power by the Assyrians.

Remember the feelings and attitudes in the poem

1) **CALM** — The destruction of the Assyrian army is described as strangely calm. Byron uses adjectives with negative prefixes, like "unlifted" and "unsmote", to emphasise how passive the soldiers are.

2) **LOSS** — The army is killed, causing a massive loss of life. The final stanza shows the Assyrians' widows crying and religious idols being destroyed. This shows that all war ends in pain and destruction.

3) **POWER** — The physical strength of the Assyrians is contrasted with the superior but calm power of God.

Go a step further and give a personal response

Have a go at answering these questions to help you come up with your own ideas about the poem:

Q1.   What is the effect of using imagery related to the natural world in the poem?

Q2.   Why do you think the poet has not made the Angel of Death a violent figure?

Q3.   Do you think the speaker wants us to sympathise with the "widows of Ashur"? Why / why not?

Conflict in wartime, effects of conflict, loss, nature...

'The Charge of the Light Brigade' also presents the effects of conflict on a large scale. However, you could also compare the loss in this poem with much more personal loss, such as the loss in 'Poppies'.

Extract from 'The Prelude'

Happy, rural image.

The speaker appears confident.

Oxymoron hints at the speaker's guilt.

Again, the speaker seems confident, maybe a bit arrogant. This contrasts with the mood later in the extract.

The metaphor of 'a fairy boat' makes the scene seem magical and otherworldly, but still not threatening.

Turning point (volta) introduces a complete change in tone. The simple word is emphasised by being at the start of the line and by the caesura.

The mountain is personified. Ugly image — contrast to earlier beautiful images of the boat ("elfin", "swan").

The mountain is calm, powerful and in control — contrasts with the speaker's fear.

The impact was long lasting.

The vague language shows that the speaker doesn't understand what he's seen — he's struggling to describe it.

Nature is described as a powerful, conscious being that can influence our lives.

Unclear here who "her" is. An earlier part of the poem suggests it's nature, personified.

Seems familiar to him.

The speaker knows he's doing something wrong — this is the first clue that something isn't quite right.

The succession of 'l' sounds helps the extract flow, like the boat moving gently across the lake.

This emptiness contrasts with line 22, when he looks at the horizon again. This makes the appearance of the mountain more shocking.

The natural simile shows that he's confident and in control — enhances the contrast with the next line.

Very different language is used to describe the mountain — darker and more threatening.

The repetition of sibilant sounds creates a sinister mood.

He's afraid and guilty, and wants to hide away — he feels like an intruder.

The event has had a big impact on him — 'grave' means serious, but may also be a reminder of his own mortality.

The speaker is left feeling alone and unsettled.

The speaker no longer thinks of nature in terms of pretty images — he's learnt there's more to it than that.

Unsettling image — helps us to empathise with him. Huge contrast to the tone and mood at start.

One summer evening (led by her) I found
A little boat tied to a willow tree
Within a rocky cave, its usual home.
Straight I unloosed her chain, and stepping in
5   Pushed from the shore. It was an act of stealth
And troubled pleasure, nor without the voice
Of mountain-echoes did my boat move on;
Leaving behind her still, on either side,
Small circles glittering idly in the moon,
10   Until they melted all into one track
Of sparkling light. But now, like one who rows,
Proud of his skill, to reach a chosen point
With an unswerving line, I fixed my view
Upon the summit of a craggy ridge,
15   The horizon's utmost boundary; far above
Was nothing but the stars and the grey sky.
She was an elfin pinnace; lustily
I dipped my oars into the silent lake,
And, as I rose upon the stroke, my boat
20   Went heaving through the water like a swan;
When, from behind that craggy steep till then
The horizon's bound, a huge peak, black and huge,
As if with voluntary power instinct,
Upreared its head. I struck and struck again,
25   And growing still in stature the grim shape
Towered up between me and the stars, and still,
For so it seemed, with purpose of its own
And measured motion like a living thing,
Strode after me. With trembling oars I turned,
30   And through the silent water stole my way
Back to the covert of the willow tree;
There in her mooring-place I left my bark, –
And through the meadows homeward went, in grave
And serious mood; but after I had seen
35   That spectacle, for many days, my brain
Worked with a dim and undetermined sense
Of unknown modes of being; o'er my thoughts
There hung a darkness, call it solitude
Or blank desertion. No familiar shapes
40   Remained, no pleasant images of trees,
Of sea or sky, no colours of green fields;
But huge and mighty forms, that do not live
Like living men, moved slowly through the mind
By day, and were a trouble to my dreams.

Context — 'The Prelude'
This is an extract from the first of fourteen books that make up Wordsworth's poem, 'The Prelude'. The book is entitled 'Introduction — Childhood and School-Time'. Wordsworth was a Romantic poet (see p.5). Like other Romantic poetry, this extract explores the connection between nature and human emotion, and the way human identity and character is shaped by experience.

POEM DICTIONARY
stealth — secrecy
pinnace — a small boat
lustily — enthusiastically
covert — shelter
bark — an old type of sailing boat

William Wordsworth

William Wordsworth was a poet from the Lake District. 'The Prelude' is an autobiographical poem — it explores key moments and experiences in Wordsworth's life. It was published shortly after his death in 1850.

You've got to know what the poem's about

1) The extract begins on a summer evening when the speaker finds a <u>boat</u> tied to a tree. He <u>unties</u> the boat and takes it out on the <u>lake</u>.

2) Initially the speaker seems <u>happy</u> and <u>confident</u>, and he describes a beautiful scene. A <u>mountain</u> appears on the horizon and the speaker is <u>afraid</u> of its <u>size</u> and <u>power</u>.

3) He turns the boat around and goes home, but his view of nature has <u>changed</u>.

The mountain scared Bill, but he wasn't sure why.

Learn about the form, structure and language

1) **FORM** — This extract is a <u>first-person narrative</u>. It sounds personal and describes a turning point in the poet's life. The use of <u>blank verse</u> (unrhymed verse in <u>iambic pentameter</u>) makes it sound serious and important, and the <u>regular rhythm</u> makes it sound like <u>natural speech</u>.

2) **STRUCTURE** — There are three main sections in the extract. In the first, the <u>tone</u> is fairly <u>light</u> and <u>carefree</u>. There's a <u>distinct change</u> when the mountain appears — the tone becomes <u>darker</u> and more <u>fearful</u>. In the final section, the speaker <u>reflects</u> on how the experience has <u>changed</u> him.

3) **BEAUTIFUL LANGUAGE** — The extract begins with a series of <u>pretty</u>, <u>pastoral images</u> of nature.

4) **CONFIDENT LANGUAGE** — The speaker appears <u>sure</u> of himself at first — almost <u>arrogant</u> in his view of himself and his place in the world. He gives the impression of feeling <u>powerful</u>.

5) **DRAMATIC LANGUAGE** — The initial glimpses of <u>threatening</u> language become more <u>intense</u> after the <u>mountain</u> appears. The speaker comes to understand how <u>powerful</u> nature is.

6) **FEARFUL LANGUAGE** — The speaker is far <u>less confident</u> at the end of the extract. He's troubled by the "huge and mighty forms" of nature he's glimpsed. The experience has a lasting, <u>haunting</u> effect on him.

Remember the feelings and attitudes in the poem

1) **CONFIDENCE** — The speaker feels <u>comfortable</u> and <u>in control</u> to start with, but his confidence <u>in himself</u> and the <u>world around him</u> is <u>shaken</u> by this one event.

2) **FEAR** — Nature is shown to be more <u>powerful</u> than a human being. The speaker is left with a feeling of <u>awe</u> and <u>respect</u> for nature, but he's also <u>scared</u> by it.

3) **REFLECTION** — The poem <u>ends</u> with the speaker reflecting on how he's been <u>changed</u> by the event. His <u>thoughts</u> and <u>dreams</u> are still <u>troubled</u> by what he's experienced.

Go a step further and give a personal response

Have a go at <u>answering</u> these <u>questions</u> to help you come up with <u>your own ideas</u> about the extract:

Q1.   What does "troubled pleasure" (line 6) suggest about the speaker's actions and feelings?

Q2.   What is the effect of the repetition of "and" in lines 24-29?

Q3.   Can you empathise with the speaker? Is his reaction understandable?

Q4.   What impression of nature do you have by the end of the extract?

KEY THEMES

Nature, individual experiences, fear, memory...

Nature is also presented as being a very powerful and frightening force in 'Exposure'. The speakers of 'Cousin Kate' and 'War Photographer' have also been changed by their unique, individual experiences.

The Man He Killed

The whole poem is written in speech marks — this makes the reader imagine someone speaking to them directly, which makes the poem feel more personal.

No one is named in the poem — this makes it seem universal.

It's implied that the poem is set in a pub. This pleasant everyday setting contrasts with the battlefield.

Informal, colloquial language shows that he's an ordinary man — it's like he's talking to a friend.

He associates himself with the enemy and puts them on an equal footing. This implies it was just down to luck who died.

The infantry were both more likely to be working class and be killed.

Very simple, straightforward description of a dramatic event.

Repeats "I shot" from line 7 — it's as if he is replaying the scenario in his head.

Repetition of "because" shows he's stumbling to think of a reason why he killed the man.

Immediately doubts himself — he questions whether the man was really his foe. Enjambment mimics the speaker looking back to reconsider his actions.

Repetition of "my foe" shows that he is trying to convince himself that what he did was right.

Thinks the man he killed didn't deserve to die — he imagines that the man was just unemployed, like him and joined the army because he needed work.

Shortened, colloquial version of 'enlist' (to join the army).

Dashes disrupt the poem's rhythm, showing his hesitation and doubt.

Last stanza summarises the message of the poem. It's worded almost like it's a joke, but there's a sense of bitterness in it.

Rhyming "war is" with "bar is" links the ideas together — emphasising the poem's sense of irony.

Uses second-person direct address to suggest that everyone would do the same thing in a battle situation.

The juxtaposition of "shoot" and "fellow" highlights how the speaker speaks about the horrors of war in a very matter-of-fact and colloquial way.

'Had he and I but met
By some old ancient inn,
We should have sat us down to wet
Right many a nipperkin!

5 'But ranged as infantry,
And staring face to face,
I shot at him as he at me,
And killed him in his place.

'I shot him dead because –
10 Because he was my foe,
Just so: my foe of course he was;
That's clear enough; although

'He thought he'd 'list, perhaps,
Off-hand like – just as I –
15 Was out of work – had sold his traps –
No other reason why.

'Yes; quaint and curious war is!
You shoot a fellow down
You'd treat if met where any bar is,
20 Or help to half-a-crown.'

Context — The Second Boer War (1899-1902)
This poem was written at the end of the Second Boer War. Hardy was against the war, in which the British invaded the territories of Dutch settlers in what is now South Africa.

POEM DICTIONARY
to wet — to drink
nipperkin — a small amount of beer or liquor
infantry — foot soldiers
foe — enemy
traps — belongings
half-a-crown — a half crown was an old British coin

Thomas Hardy

Thomas Hardy was a very well-known English novelist and poet. He came from a working-class family, and often touched on themes such as social inequality and war, like in this poem from 1902.

You've got to know what the poem's about

1) A soldier says that he and his enemy may have been <u>friends</u> if they had met in an <u>inn</u> rather than on the battlefield. However, because they met in battle, they <u>shot</u> at each other and the other man was <u>killed</u>.

2) He imagines that the man he killed may have been very <u>similar</u> to him — he wonders whether, like him, the man only enlisted in the army because he <u>needed work</u>.

3) In the last stanza, he sums up the message of the poem. He says that war is a <u>strange</u> business — you <u>kill</u> people you might have been friends with in <u>different circumstances</u>.

Learn about the form, structure and language

1) **FORM** — The poem is a <u>dramatic monologue</u> — it's a speech from a single character. The regular <u>metre</u> and <u>rhyme scheme</u> (ABAB) make the poem <u>conversational</u>, contrasting with the poem's dark <u>subject matter</u>. The longer <u>third line</u> of each stanza is a feature of <u>short metre</u>, which is often used in <u>hymns</u>.

2) **STRUCTURE** — The <u>cyclical structure</u> of the poem reflects the speaker's thought processes as he replays his memories of the war. The "bar" in the final stanza links back to the "ancient inn" from the first stanza — this suggests that the speaker's post-war trauma is <u>ongoing</u>.

3) **COLLOQUIAL LANGUAGE** — <u>Informal</u> language and slang are used to suggest that the speaker is an ordinary, working-class man. This contrasts with the harrowing themes of <u>war</u> and <u>death</u>.

4) **MATTER-OF-FACT LANGUAGE** — The soldier uses fairly matter-of-fact, <u>unemotional</u> language to describe <u>killing</u> the man. This detached language <u>contrasts</u> with the serious message behind the poem and helps to highlight the <u>impersonal</u> nature of war.

5) **HESITANT LANGUAGE** — <u>Repetition</u> and caesurae are used to show that the speaker is <u>questioning</u> why he shot the man. This is in <u>contrast</u> to the final paragraph, where the exclamation "Yes" suggests that he's come to a <u>conclusion</u>.

Remember the feelings and attitudes in the poem

1) **GUILT** — It's not immediately <u>obvious</u> that the speaker feels <u>guilty</u>. However, the <u>shift in focus</u> between the third and fourth stanzas suggests that he's having doubts about whether he was right to kill his "foe".

2) **IRONY** — The soldier acknowledges that there's a <u>sense of irony</u> about the situation — he's killed a man who he might have been friends with in different circumstances.

3) **TRAGEDY** — By showing the <u>similarities</u> between the speaker and the "foe", Hardy is making a point about the <u>tragedy of war</u> and how there's a sense of <u>pointlessness</u> to it.

Go a step further and give a personal response

Have a go at <u>answering</u> these <u>questions</u> to help you come up with <u>your own ideas</u> about the poem:

Q1.   Do you think the speaker regrets what he has done? Why / why not?
Q2.   Why do you think the poet uses a mix of friendly and unemotional language in the poem?
Q3.   Why do you think the speaker describes war as "quaint and curious" on line 17?

Conflict in wartime, reality of conflict, memory...

The reality of conflict is a key theme in 'Belfast Confetti', 'The Charge of the Light Brigade' and 'Exposure'. 'Poppies' and 'The Prelude' both present the memories of speakers affected by conflict.

Cousin Kate

Pastoral, countryside imagery emphasises her innocence.

The first stanza gives the impression that the poem's not going to end well — anaphora and rhetorical questions are used to show her despair.

Sounds like she is being hunted by the lord.

Treated as a toy for the lord's entertainment. This shows her powerlessness and lack of control over her own fate.

Mocks Kate by calling her "Lady Kate". It is clear she doesn't have respect for her. Exclamation emphasises how strongly she feels towards Kate.

Anaphora — "He" followed by verbs makes the lord seem predatory. It gives the impression that Kate is passive and that he has power over her.

All of the actions are done by the lord to the women, showing that they are both passive.

Suggests that Kate is no more of a moral person than the speaker — she only succeeded because she is stronger.

The speaker is shown to be unreliable — earlier she says that her love for the lord was "true", but here she says she wouldn't have betrayed her cousin and would have spat at the lord.

Shift in tone — there's a bittersweet sense of satisfaction because, as Kate seems unlikely to produce an heir, the speaker's son is likely to inherit the lord's wealth.

Repetition and alliteration show how important the child is to her and suggests a sense of desperation to keep him close.

I was a cottage-maiden
   Hardened by sun and air,
Contented with my cottage-mates,
   Not mindful I was fair.
5 Why did a great lord find me out
   And praise my flaxen hair?
Why did a great lord find me out
   To fill my heart with care?

He lured me to his palace-home —
10   Woe's me for joy thereof —
To lead a shameless shameful life,
   His plaything and his love.
He wore me like a golden knot,
   He changed me like a glove:
15 So now I moan an unclean thing
   Who might have been a dove.

O Lady Kate, my Cousin Kate,
   You grow more fair than I:
He saw you at your father's gate,
20   Chose you and cast me by.
He watched your steps along the lane,
   Your sport among the rye:
He lifted you from mean estate
   To sit with him on high.

25 Because you were so good and pure
   He bound you with his ring:
The neighbours call you good and pure,
   Call me an outcast thing.
Even so I sit and howl in dust
30   You sit in gold and sing:
Now which of us has tenderer heart?
   You had the stronger wing.

O Cousin Kate, my love was true,
   Your love was writ in sand:
35 If he had fooled not me but you,
   If you stood where I stand,
He had not won me with his love
   Nor bought me with his land:
I would have spit into his face
40   And not have taken his hand.

Yet I've a gift you have not got
   And seem not like to get:
For all your clothes and wedding-ring
   I've little doubt you fret.
45 My fair-haired son, my shame, my pride,
   Cling closer, closer yet:
Your sire would give broad lands for one
   To wear his coronet.

She was happy with her position in life.

She is regretful of the pleasure she enjoyed at the lord's palace and starts lamenting.

Oxymoron suggests that the speaker didn't feel ashamed about her actions, even though they were considered "shameful" by society. The sibilant 'sh' sounds create a shushing sound, suggesting secrecy.

Compares herself to a luxurious, "golden" object that he wears.

She's considered "unclean" because she is no longer a virgin. This contrasts with the "dove", which is a symbol of innocence.

He married Kate because she was "pure" — she didn't have sex before marriage. Repetition of "good and pure" shows the speaker's building anger.

Uses sensory language, to contrast "dust" with "gold", and "howl" with "sing". This emphasises how the speaker's misery contrasts with Kate's happiness and luxury. Though Kate is still not treated like a person — she is likened to a songbird.

Contrasts her own, genuine love with Kate's love, which she suggests is fleeting and could be easily washed away.

Suggests that it is just chance that they're in this position and not the other way round.

Oxymoron shows her mixed feelings about the situation — she might be miserable and shamed by society, but she expresses satisfaction and pride that she has a son.

Context — Fallen women
In the 19th century, women were expected to conform to strict moral standards. Women who had sex outside of wedlock were considered to be 'fallen women' and were frowned upon by the rest of society. Rossetti spent some time volunteering with church organisations set up to help so-called 'fallen women'.

POEM DICTIONARY
flaxen — blonde
woe's me — a phrase meaning "I am sorrowful"
sport — games
rye — a type of cereal crop grown in fields
mean estate — a poor background
sire — father
coronet — a small crown

Christina Rossetti

Christina Rossetti (1830-1894) is one of the best-known poets of the Victorian era. Her poems cover themes such as Christianity and women's roles in society. 'Cousin Kate' was published in 1862.

You've got to know what the poem's about

1) A cottage-maid describes how she was seduced by a <u>rich lord</u>. He used her and <u>cast her aside</u> in favour of her cousin Kate. This caused her to lose her <u>innocent reputation</u> and become <u>rejected</u> by society.

2) The speaker continually <u>compares</u> Kate's happy life with her own <u>misery</u>. She feels <u>betrayed</u> by Kate and claims that she wouldn't have done the same if the roles were <u>reversed</u>.

3) In the last stanza, she reveals that she has a <u>son</u> with the lord and hints that Kate is <u>unable</u> to produce an heir.

"He bound me with a ring too, Kate."

Learn about the form, structure and language

1) **FORM** — The poem is a <u>dramatic monologue</u> addressed to the speaker's cousin, Kate, who she refers to as "you". The speaker is <u>unreliable</u> — her opinions of Kate are coloured by <u>resentment</u> and some of her opinions <u>contradict</u> each other.

2) **STRUCTURE** — The poem is in <u>chronological order</u>. The speaker first explains her <u>relationship</u> with the lord. She then tells the reader about Kate's <u>betrayal</u> and finally about her <u>son with the lord</u>.

3) **PASSIVE LANGUAGE** — The lord is the <u>subject</u> of many sentences (he is the one <u>doing</u> the action), while the women are the <u>objects</u> (e.g. "He wore me") — this shows their relative <u>passivity</u>. Rossetti reinforces this point by using similes to compare the women to <u>objects</u>, e.g. "like a golden knot"

4) **REPETITION** — In the second stanza, Rossetti uses <u>anaphora</u> to describe how the lord <u>seduced</u> and <u>abandoned</u> the <u>speaker</u>. It is used again in the third stanza to emphasise Kate's <u>passiveness</u>. This reflects how, although he treated the women in <u>similar ways</u>, they came to different <u>fates</u>.

5) **CONTRASTS** — The poem contrasts <u>innocence</u> and <u>corruption</u> throughout. This can be seen through the speaker's loss of reputation, as well as through the comparison of the speaker and her cousin Kate. The speaker also frequently contrasts Kate's <u>happiness</u> and <u>success</u> with her own <u>failure</u>.

Remember the feelings and attitudes in the poem

1) **INJUSTICE** — The speaker clearly feels a sense of <u>injustice</u> at the way she's been <u>treated</u> in comparison to Kate. She contrasts Kate's situation with her own to express her <u>resentment</u>.

2) **ANGER** — The speaker directs <u>anger</u> towards the lord, as well as Kate, for putting her in this <u>situation</u>.

3) **BITTERSWEET SATISFACTION** — In the final stanza, the speaker has <u>mixed feelings</u> about her situation. She is still <u>angry</u> at how she's been treated, but she expresses a sense of <u>satisfaction</u> at the fact that she, unlike Kate, has provided the lord with an <u>heir</u>.

Go a step further and give a personal response

Have a go at <u>answering</u> these <u>questions</u> to help you come up with <u>your own ideas</u> about the poem:

Q1.   What does "He changed me like a glove" show about the speaker's relationship with the lord?
Q2.   Why do you think the lord was able to get away with his actions?
Q3.   Why do you think the poem is addressed to Kate and not the lord?

KEY THEMES

Loss and suffering, anger, individual experiences...

You could compare the personal experiences of Rossetti's speaker with those of the speaker in 'The Prelude' extract, or you could compare her feelings of anger with those in 'A Poison Tree' or 'Half-caste'.

Half-caste

Excuse me
standing on one leg
I'm half-caste

> Sarcastically apologises for being "half-caste". This starts the poem with a ironic tone and gets the reader's attention.

> Addresses the reader directly — challenging them to explain their views. This is repeated multiple times for emphasis.

5
Explain yuself
wha yu mean
when you say half-caste
yu mean when picasso
mix red an green
is a half-caste canvas/

> Shows that mixing things together can create beauty.

10
explain yuself
wha yu mean
when yu say half-caste
yu mean when light an shadow
mix in de sky

> Non-standard punctuation — forward slashes usually link two ideas together, but because the lines end after these slashes it is as though the speaker is only able to make half of their point.

> Explaining that the weather is a mix of different things shows that it's natural.

15
is a half-caste weather/
well in dat case
england weather
nearly always half-caste

> Not capitalising the 'e' in "england" could show a lack of respect.

> The use of Caribbean dialect shows that the speaker is proud of their mixed heritage.

> Plays on the word 'cast' to create humour and reinforce their point.

20
in fact some o dem cloud
half-caste till dem overcast
so spiteful dem dont want de sun pass
ah rass/

> Accuses English clouds of being "spiteful" towards the sun.

> Impolite Caribbean slang.

explain yuself
wha yu mean

25
when you say half-caste
yu mean tchaikovsky
sit down at dah piano
an mix a black key
wid a white key

> Repeating this refrain continues the poem's confrontational tone.

30
is a half-caste symphony/

> Piano music uses a mixture of black and white keys, but people don't call it "half-caste", so the speaker questions why mixed race people are described as such.

> Uses humour again to present the mixing of things positively.

Explain yuself
wha yu mean
Ah listening to yu wid de keen
half of mih ear

35
Ah lookin at yu wid de keen
half of mih eye
and when I'm introduced to yu
I'm sure you'll understand
why I offer yu half-a-hand

> Uses humorous imagery to expose how ridiculous the term "half-caste" is.

> Juxtaposing standard English with Guyanese dialect shows that mixing dialects can create poetry.

40
an when I sleep at night
I close half-a-eye
consequently when I dream
I dream half-a-dream
an when moon begin to glow

> Metaphors take the term "half-caste" and apply it to body parts, which shows that using the term implies that mixed-race people are incomplete.

> The image of the speaker only casting "half-a-shadow" gives a supernatural feel and plays on the idea that "half-caste" people aren't complete human beings.

45
I half-caste human being
cast half-a-shadow
but yu must come back tomorrow
wid de whole of yu eye
an de whole of yu ear

> Likening the term "half-caste" to "half-a-dream" reinforces the absurdity of the term, as it is impossible to dream "half-a-dream".

> Draws attention to the homophone "cast", which can mean 'to form' — therefore "half-caste" can sound like it means 'half-formed'.

50
an de whole of yu mind

> The word "but" marks a turning point in poem. Here, the speaker adopts a more serious tone, advising the reader to come back more open-minded.

> Uses short lines (almost half-lines) to give the poem a concise and powerful ending.

an I will tell yu
de other half
of my story

> The lack of a full stop highlights that their "story" is unfinished.

POEM DICTIONARY
half-caste — an outdated and offensive word for mixed race
ah rass — Caribbean slang used to express anger
Picasso — a famous painter
Tchaikovsky — a famous composer

John Agard

John Agard was born in Guyana, a Caribbean country in South America. He is of mixed race — his father is Guyanese and his mother is Portuguese. He moved to the UK in 1977 and wrote 'Half-caste' in 1996.

You've got to know what the poem's about

1) The speaker asks the reader to <u>think</u> about what the term "half-caste" means. They use metaphors to draw attention to the way society calls <u>mixed-race people</u> "half-caste", but they don't they do the same for everything that's <u>mixed</u>, like great paintings, the weather and classical music.

2) They find no <u>logic</u> in the term "half-caste" and <u>challenge</u> people to explain their way of thinking. They <u>mock</u> the term by talking about 'halves' of other things to show that it doesn't <u>make sense</u>.

3) They say people should <u>open</u> their eyes and minds, and think about the language they are using.

Learn about the form, structure and language

1) **FORM** — There's no <u>regular</u> rhyme scheme, but <u>rhymes</u> and <u>half-rhymes</u> are used to create a sense of <u>rhythm</u>. The use of <u>enjambment</u> and a lack of <u>standard punctuation</u> gives the poem a sense of <u>urgency</u>.

2) **STRUCTURE** — The first half of the poem contains a series of <u>metaphors</u> that compare being <u>mixed race</u> to great art and natural weather. In the second half of the poem, the speaker <u>exaggerates</u> the idea that he is half a person to expose the <u>ridiculousness</u> of the term "half-caste". The final lines invite the reader to open their mind up and <u>reconsider</u> any thoughts they might have had about the term "half-caste".

3) **METAPHOR** — The speaker likens being mixed race to great art that was created by mixing things. This suggests that mixing things creates something <u>beautiful</u>, rather than something <u>incomplete</u>.

4) **DIALECT** — By using Guyanese <u>dialect</u> words and <u>creole language</u> (a mix of English and other languages) alongside <u>Standard English</u>, Agard shows how mixing things can create powerful <u>poetry</u>.

5) **CONFRONTATIONAL LANGUAGE** — The poem is addressed <u>directly</u> to the reader — "yu" and "I" are used a lot — this makes it <u>conversational</u>, but also confrontational. The speaker challenges <u>assumptions</u> by repeatedly saying "Explain yuself".

6) **HUMOROUS LANGUAGE** — Despite the speaker's <u>confrontational</u> attitude, the poem has a <u>humorous</u> tone. The prefix "half-" is added before various words to reveal the <u>absurdity</u> of the term "half-caste".

Remember the feelings and attitudes in the poem

1) **ANGER** — <u>Confrontational language</u> shows the speaker's anger at being called "half-caste". They think it's an <u>offensive term</u> and use a variety of imagery to show the reader why they shouldn't use it.

2) **SARCASM** — The poem has a <u>sarcastic tone</u> throughout. This creates <u>humour</u> and adds more <u>power</u> to the speaker's arguments, as it provides them with <u>intelligence</u> and <u>wit</u>.

Go a step further and give a personal response

Have a go at <u>answering</u> these <u>questions</u> to help you come up with <u>your own ideas</u> about the poem:

Q1. What is the effect of the poem being written in the first person?
Q2. Why do you think the speaker repeats the word "half-caste" multiple times?
Q3. Why do you think the poem doesn't end with a full stop?

Identity, anger, conflict in society...

You could compare the speaker's anger with that of the speaker in 'A Poison Tree' or 'The Class Game'. The formation of identity is also a key theme in 'The Class Game', as well as in 'No Problem' and 'Catrin'.

Exposure

This is a shared, painful experience.

Nature is personified and seems to be attacking them.

Lots of different emotions — another reason why their brains hurt.

Our brains ache, in the merciless iced east winds that knive us...
Wearied we keep awake because the night is silent...
Low, drooping flares confuse our memory of the salient...
Worried by silence, sentries whisper, curious, nervous,
5   But nothing happens.

Ellipses hint that they're waiting for something to happen — it never does.

The "brambles" of the barbed wire remind us of the pain caused by nature.

The short, simple half-line emphasises their boredom and tension.

Watching, we hear the mad gusts tugging on the wire,
Like twitching agonies of men among its brambles.
Northward, incessantly, the flickering gunnery rumbles,
Far off, like a dull rumour of some other war.
10   What are we doing here?

This is a Biblical reference to Matthew 24:6, where Jesus foretells the end of the world. He says "You will hear of wars and rumours of wars".

Rhetorical question asks what the point of it all is.

The poignant misery of dawn begins to grow...
We only know war lasts, rain soaks, and clouds sag stormy.
Dawn massing in the east her melancholy army
Attacks once more in ranks on shivering ranks of grey,
15   But nothing happens.

Dawn is personified using the language of battle. Normally dawn brings hope, but not here.

Sibilance mimics the whistling sound of bullets flying.

Grey was also the colour of German uniforms, so this aligns nature with the enemy.

Sudden successive flights of bullets streak the silence.
Less deathly than the air that shudders black with snow,
With sidelong flowing flakes that flock, pause, and renew;
We watch them wandering up and down the wind's nonchalance,
20   But nothing happens.

Alliteration emphasises the relentlessness of the snow.

Snow is normally white (symbolising purity), but here it's black (symbolising evil or death).

The snowflakes are personified — they're maliciously seeking the men's faces.

Pale flakes with fingering stealth come feeling for our faces –
We cringe in holes, back on forgotten dreams, and stare, snow-dazed,
Deep into grassier ditches. So we drowse, sun-dozed,
Littered with blossoms trickling where the blackbird fusses,
25   – Is it that we are dying?

Half-rhyme creates a link between their current situation and their dreams of the past.

Another question, possibly answering the first question — they're here to die.

Slowly our ghosts drag home: glimpsing the sunk fires, glozed
With crusted dark-red jewels; crickets jingle there;
For hours the innocent mice rejoice: the house is theirs;
Shutters and doors, all closed: on us the doors are closed, –
30   We turn back to our dying.

Assonance of long 'oh' sounds makes the imagined journey sound painful and slow.

Suggests that they believe they're sacrificing themselves in order for life at home to be preserved.

Since we believe not otherwise can kind fires burn;
Nor ever suns smile true on child, or field, or fruit.
For God's invincible spring our love is made afraid;
Therefore, not loath, we lie out here; therefore were born,
35   For love of God seems dying.

The caesurae in this stanza create a division on each line, which reflects how the men are shut out of their homes. This also reflects the soldiers' concern that people back home were losing interest in their fate as the war dragged on.

Could mean that their love of God is disappearing, or that they feel God's love for them is dying.

Tonight, this frost will fasten on this mud and us,
Shrivelling many hands, puckering foreheads crisp.
The burying-party, picks and shovels in shaking grasp,
Pause over half-known faces. All their eyes are ice,
40   But nothing happens.

Vivid image of what exposure to the cold does to their bodies.

Metaphor refers to the eyes of the living and the dead men — it's a vivid description of how they've been overpowered by nature. It hints that the living men are no longer able to feel any emotion.

Final stanza ends in same way as first stanza, suggesting that even death doesn't change anything.

POEM DICTIONARY
salient — a section of trenches that reached into enemy territory
sentries — soldiers watching for danger
poignant — painfully sad
nonchalance — casual lack of concern
glozed — a combination of 'glowing' and 'glazed'
loath — unwilling
puckering — contracting into wrinkles or folds

Wilfred Owen

Wilfred Owen wrote 'Exposure' in 1917-18 from the trenches of World War One, not long before he was killed in battle. Much of Owen's poetry reveals his anger at the war's waste of life and its horrific conditions.

You've got to know what the poem's about

1) Soldiers in the trenches of World War One are awake at night, afraid of an enemy attack.

2) However, nature seems to be their main enemy — it's freezing cold, windy and snowing.

3) The men imagine returning home, but the doors there are closed to them. They believe that sacrificing themselves in the war is the only way of keeping their loved ones at home safe.

4) They return to thinking about their deaths in the icy, bleak trenches.

Learn about the form, structure and language

1) **FORM** — The poem's written in the present tense using the first person plural (e.g. "Our", "We", "us"). This collective voice shows how the experience was shared by soldiers across the war. Each stanza has a regular rhyme scheme (ABBAC), reflecting the monotonous nature of the men's experience, but rhymes are often half-rhymes (e.g. "snow" & "renew"). The rhyme scheme offers no comfort or satisfaction — the rhymes are jagged like the reality of the men's experience and reflect their confusion and fading energy. Each stanza ends with a half-line, leaving a gap which mirrors the lack of activity or hope for the men.

2) **STRUCTURE** — The poem has eight stanzas, but there's no real progression — the last stanza ends with the same words as the first one, reflecting the monotony of life in the trenches and the absence of change.

3) **QUESTIONS** — The poem uses rhetorical questions to ask why the men are exposed to such dreadful conditions, and whether there's any point to their suffering.

4) **PERSONIFICATION** — Nature is repeatedly personified, making it seem the real enemy in the war.

5) **BLEAK LANGUAGE** — The poem includes lots of bleak imagery to remind the reader of the men's pain, the awful weather and the lack of hope for the soldiers. Assonance, onomatopoeia and carefully chosen verbs add to the bleak mood and make the descriptions vivid and distressing.

Remember the feelings and attitudes in the poem

1) **SUFFERING** — There are reminders of the real, physical pain that the soldiers experience, as well as their exhaustion and fatigue. Even thinking about home is painful for the men as they're not welcome there.

2) **BOREDOM** — There's a sense of frustration at their situation — they are "Worried", "Watching" and waiting, but "nothing happens" and the men are left to contemplate their own deaths.

3) **HOPELESSNESS** — The soldiers are helpless against the power of nature and there is nothing they can do to change their situation. The poem offers little hope of a future for the men.

Go a step further and give a personal response

Have a go at answering these questions to help you come up with your own ideas about the poem:

Q1.   What do you think the title is referring to? Could it have more than one meaning?

Q2.   Do you think the men are relieved about a new day dawning? How can you tell?

Q3.   Why do you think the word "ghosts" is used to describe the men thinking about going home?

Reality of conflict, nature, loss and suffering...

Compare how Owen describes the reality of conflict with how Carson describes it in 'Belfast Confetti'. You could also compare the theme of loss and suffering with that found in 'What Were They Like?'.

The Charge of the Light Brigade

The rhythm sounds like galloping horses' hooves — it gives the impression that the horses are unstoppable.

They're presented as one group with one purpose.

Soldiers realise the order was a mistake but do what they're told because it's their duty to obey orders. The poet respects them for this.

There's a line in the Bible that says "Yea, though I walk through the valley of the shadow of death, I will fear no evil" (Psalm 23). Using Biblical references makes the poem seem solemn and significant.

The first three stanzas end with the same line. It adds to the sense of foreboding and reminds us of the number of soldiers.

This reminds us that the cavalry only had swords against the Russian guns.

Several lines begin with verbs, emphasising the action and increasing the pace of the poem.

The repetition of "not" emphasises the fact that some of the brigade have been killed. It also creates a broken, stuttering effect, making it sound almost as if the speaker is upset.

Similar to the opening lines of stanza 3, but now the soldiers are retreating.

The repetition of "left of" reminds us that lives have been lost, and makes the poem sound sad.

This is a rhetorical question that challenges the reader.

This command is repeated to leave the reader with the idea that they should honour the cavalry.

Half a league, half a league,
    Half a league onward,
All in the valley of Death
    Rode the six hundred.
5 'Forward, the Light Brigade!
Charge for the guns!' he said:
Into the valley of Death
    Rode the six hundred.

'Forward, the Light Brigade!'
10 Was there a man dismay'd?
Not tho' the soldier knew
    Some one had blunder'd:
Theirs not to make reply,
Theirs not to reason why,
15 Theirs but to do and die:
Into the valley of Death
    Rode the six hundred.

Cannon to right of them,
Cannon to left of them,
20 Cannon in front of them
    Volley'd and thunder'd;
Storm'd at with shot and shell,
Boldly they rode and well,
Into the jaws of Death,
25 Into the mouth of Hell
    Rode the six hundred.

Flash'd all their sabres bare,
Flash'd as they turn'd in air
Sabring the gunners there,
30 Charging an army, while
    All the world wonder'd:
Plunged in the battery-smoke
Right thro' the line they broke;
Cossack and Russian
35 Reel'd from the sabre-stroke
    Shatter'd and sunder'd.
Then they rode back, but not
    Not the six hundred.

Cannon to right of them,
40 Cannon to left of them,
Cannon behind them
    Volley'd and thunder'd;
Storm'd at with shot and shell,
While horse and hero fell,
45 They that had fought so well
Came thro' the jaws of Death
Back from the mouth of Hell,
All that was left of them,
    Left of six hundred.

50 When can their glory fade?
O the wild charge they made!
    All the world wonder'd.
Honour the charge they made!
Honour the Light Brigade,
55   Noble six hundred!

Sounds sinister — the reader is warned right from the start that something bad is going to happen.

The commanding officer is speaking here.

Rhyme and repetition emphasise the soldiers' obedience and sense of duty, even though they know they will almost certainly be killed.

Repetition at the start and end of the lines reflects the way the soldiers are surrounded by the enemy's guns. It also replicates the sound of gunfire.

Sibilance emphasises the idea of ammunition flying towards them.

These images personify death and hell and make them seem like monsters that the soldiers can't escape from.

The repetition of "Flash'd" and the rhyme create a powerful image of the cavalry using their swords.

Double meaning — could mean that people marvelled at their bravery or that they wondered why they had been sent on the charge. This poem was written in 1854 in response to a newspaper article about the battle. Many newspapers at the time were critical of the Crimean War, but this poem focuses on the bravery of the soldiers rather than the mistakes of the military leaders.

The sibilance here sounds vicious.

Powerful, onomatopoeic verbs suggest the noise from the cannons.

The sense of admiration is touched with sadness.

Sounds dramatic and daring.

POEM DICTIONARY
sabres — long curved swords
sabring — to cut or wound with a sabre
battery — a group of cannons
Cossack — a warrior from southern Russia and Ukraine
sunder'd — broken into pieces

Alfred Tennyson

Alfred Tennyson was one of the greatest poets of the Victorian era, and was Poet Laureate from 1850 until his death in 1892. He wrote this poem in 1854 as a tribute to the men who died in the battle it describes.

You've got to know what the poem's about

1) The poem describes a disastrous <u>battle</u> between <u>British cavalry</u> (soldiers on horseback) and <u>Russian forces</u> during the <u>Crimean War</u> (1853-1856).

2) A <u>misunderstanding</u> meant that the Light Brigade were ordered to <u>advance</u> into a valley surrounded by <u>enemy soldiers</u>.

3) The cavalry were only armed with <u>swords</u>, whereas the Russian soldiers had <u>guns</u>. The Light Brigade were virtually <u>defenceless</u> against their enemies, and many of them were <u>killed</u>.

Learn about the form, structure and language

1) **FORM** — The poem's narrated in the <u>third person</u>, making it seem like a <u>story</u>. The regular, relentless <u>rhythm</u> creates a fast pace, imitating the cavalry's advance and the <u>energy</u> of the battle. Rhyming <u>couplets</u> and <u>triplets</u> drive the poem forwards, but the momentum is <u>broken</u> by unrhymed lines, which could mirror the <u>horses stumbling</u> and <u>soldiers falling</u>. The overall lack of rhyme scheme hints at the <u>chaos</u> of war.

2) **STRUCTURE** — The poem tells the story of the battle in <u>chronological order</u>, from the <u>charge</u> of the men in the first three stanzas, to the <u>battle</u> in the fourth and the <u>retreat</u> in the fifth. The final stanza is shorter and <u>summarises</u> the <u>heroism</u> of the brigade.

3) **REPETITION** — Repetition creates a sense of <u>impending doom</u> and <u>inevitability</u>. Repetition of "<u>six hundred</u>" at the end of each stanza reinforces the idea of the <u>large numbers</u> of men involved, with the references to them <u>summarising</u> the story of the <u>battle</u>.

4) **HEROIC LANGUAGE** — Adverbs like "<u>Boldly</u>" and verbs like "<u>Charging</u>" emphasise the men's <u>bravery</u>. <u>Respectful</u> language shows how the speaker feels the soldiers should be <u>remembered</u>.

5) **VIOLENT LANGUAGE** — The speaker chooses <u>powerful</u> verbs and adjectives to give a strong sense of the <u>violence</u> of the battle, and uses <u>sounds</u> to create a vivid, noisy, <u>hellish</u> setting.

Remember the feelings and attitudes in the poem

1) **ADMIRATION** — The speaker admires the <u>bravery</u> and <u>sacrifice</u> of the men because they <u>obeyed orders</u> even though they knew death was likely. He thinks that the world should <u>recognise</u> their bravery and <u>appreciate</u> their sacrifice.

Derek was relieved his horse hadn't learnt how to charge yet.

2) **PATRIOTISM** — The men followed the orders because of their <u>duty</u> to their <u>country</u>, and the speaker portrays them as <u>heroes</u> for doing this.

3) **HORROR** — There's a suggestion that the speaker is horrified by the <u>violence</u> of the battle.

Go a step further and give a personal response

Have a go at <u>answering</u> these <u>questions</u> to help you come up with <u>your own ideas</u> about the poem:

Q1.	How does the phrase "jaws of Death" (line 46) make you feel? Explain your answer.
Q2.	How does the speaker convey the terror and violence of the battle?
Q3.	Why do you think the stanzas in the poem are different lengths?

Conflict in wartime, effects of conflict, reality of conflict...

'Poppies' and 'What Were They Like?' are good poems to look at alongside this one if you're thinking about the effects of conflict. 'The Man He Killed' and 'Exposure' work well for the reality of conflict.

Catrin

Although the poem is autobiographical, the use of personal pronouns makes it relatable to any mother-child relationship.

The addition of "child" here is unusually formal. It seems as though speaker is trying to distance herself through her language.

Alliteration in this long first sentence creates a sense of monotony, which emphasises the speaker's impatience as she waited in the hospital.

Repeats the first line to stress the importance of this memory.

The repeated 'f' sounds are alliterative. The letters are forced out of the reader's mouth, emphasising the forceful nature of the conflict.

"Red" symbolises love and passion, but also blood and danger. This reflects the relationship between the mother and child — loving but potentially destructive.

A "rope" indicates they have been bound together, which is literal (an umbilical cord) and figurative (an emotional bond).

Implies her language was rude if it "coloured" the walls — this link to 'colourful language' highlights the intensity of giving birth.

Seems cold and medical. The birth itself is not shown as loving — it is difficult and clinical.

This oxymoron sums up their relationship — it is "tender" and loving, but at times turbulent and "wild". The word "circles" also suggests a cycle, like this kind of love is a natural part of life.

"Separate" is separated from the sentence it is a part of. The form of the sentence emphasises its meaning.

I can remember you, child,
As I stood in a hot, white
Room at the window watching
The people and cars taking
5   Turn at the traffic lights.
I can remember you, our first
Fierce confrontation, the tight
Red rope of love which we both
Fought over. It was a square
10 Environmental blank, disinfected
Of paintings or toys. I wrote
All over the walls with my
Words, coloured the clean squares
With the wild, tender circles
15 Of our struggle to become
Separate. We want, we shouted,
To be two, to be ourselves.

The change from "I" to "We" suggests that, ironically, they had to work together to come apart.

Caesurae and end-stopping mimic the struggle to breathe during childbirth.

Neither won nor lost the struggle
In the glass tank clouded with feelings
20 Which changed us both. Still I am fighting
You off, as you stand there
With your straight, strong, long
Brown hair and your rosy,
Defiant glare, bringing up
25 From the heart's pool that old rope,
Tightening about my life,
Trailing love and conflict,
As you ask may you skate
In the dark, for one more hour.

The shift to the present tense shows that the struggle is still ongoing — it never really ended. They will always be at odds about something, no matter how old they get.

The "glass tank" could refer to a medical incubator — suggests a difficult birth.

The juxtaposition of "love" and "conflict" highlights the tension between the poem's two key feelings. The word "Tightening" implies constriction, showing that this conflict is uncomfortable.

The description of the daughter resembles that of a rope — this suggests that they still have that strong connection.

Suggests a well or reservoir of love that the daughter can draw from. Repeated reference to the "rope", which is now "old", shows their long-lasting connection.

The daughter doesn't seem to understand the dangers of skating in the dark. Her innocence leaves her figuratively 'in the dark'. The change from the bright colours mentioned earlier in the poem to "the dark" also emphasises the growing separation between mother and daughter.

Their all-carrot diet helped Tim and Flopsy skate through the night.

Gillian Clarke

Gillian Clarke was born in 1937 in Cardiff. Many of her poems reflect her cultural identity and family relationships in Wales. 'Catrin' was published in 1997, and explores Clarke's relationship with her daughter.

You've got to know what the poem's about

1) A mother <u>remembers</u> when her daughter was born. Her <u>memories</u> are described in <u>vivid detail</u> — from waiting in the hospital room to the <u>violent struggle</u> of the birth itself.

2) She compares this to another <u>conflict</u> with her daughter, who is now a teenager and has asked if she can stay outside late to skate in the dark.

3) In both memories, there's a sense that the mother and daughter want to be <u>separate</u> from each other. Despite this, the mother knows their <u>bond</u> is too strong for them to <u>ever</u> be <u>completely separated</u>.

Learn about the form, structure and language

1) **FORM** — The poem is written in <u>free verse</u> — it doesn't have a regular <u>rhyme scheme</u> or <u>rhythm</u>. This makes the emotion of the poem feel <u>authentic</u>, as though the speaker is working through her thoughts and memories as they occur. <u>Enjambment</u> also helps to imitate her <u>flowing</u> thoughts as most lines run on without being end-stopped. It also reflects the "rope of love" — the <u>persisting link</u> between the pair.

2) **STRUCTURE** — The poem is split into <u>two stanzas</u> — the first covers the daughter's birth and the second looks at a later confrontation. The <u>break</u> between stanzas represents <u>time passing</u> and the girl <u>growing up</u>.

3) **LANGUAGE ABOUT CONFLICT** — The poem presents the relationship between the mother and daughter as <u>challenging</u>. The birth is described as a "<u>Fierce confrontation</u>", and later, the mother is still "<u>fighting</u>" her daughter off. Their 'battle' doesn't end — they remain locked in <u>conflict</u> throughout.

4) **LOVING LANGUAGE** — The mother's deep <u>love</u> for her daughter is shown through the poem's <u>metaphorical language</u>. The "<u>Red rope of love</u>" binds the pair together and is present throughout the poem — it <u>endures</u>, like the mother's love. The phrase "<u>heart's pool</u>" is ambiguous, allowing it to suggest a plentiful supply of <u>maternal love</u>. By showing their bond to be lasting, the poem shows how strong it is.

Remember the feelings and attitudes in the poem

1) **LOVE** — The poem explores the <u>powerful love</u> between a <u>mother</u> and her <u>daughter</u>.

2) **TENSION** — Both the mother and daughter find themselves struggling against one another at two moments in their lives. The poem also presents tension between <u>conflicted feelings</u>. The warmth of the mother's <u>love</u> is in conflict with the <u>pain</u> of giving birth and having to stop her daughter from skating.

3) **CHANGE** — The poem explores how things can <u>change</u>, while remaining <u>surprisingly similar</u>. Even though both events are years apart, they make the speaker <u>feel the same emotions</u>.

Go a step further and give a personal response

Have a go at <u>answering</u> these <u>questions</u> to help you come up with <u>your own ideas</u> about the poem:

Q1.   Why do you think the speaker mentions the cars "taking / Turn at the traffic lights"?

Q2.   What is the effect of describing the daughter's "rosy, / Defiant glare"?

Q3.   Why do you think the speaker denies her daughter the chance to continue skating?

Individual experiences, memory, identity...

This poem can be compared with the fractured family relationship in Christina Rossetti's 'Cousin Kate'. It also explores the physical and emotional separation of a mother and child as 'Poppies' does.

War Photographer

The dashes introduce examples like a bullet pointed list. The jump straight into each one is like being suddenly shown a snapshot.

Suggests not only a photo frame, but a frame of mind (a way of looking at the world).

The stability of "reassurance" is immediately undermined by the word "flexible". This reflects the ambiguity of photographs — they're open to interpretation.

Addresses the reader and society directly. Encourages people think about their own actions.

Suggests people can convince themselves that the speaker actively seeks out tragedy, rather than accepting it as part of reality.

The girls are described with so many complex adjectives that it seems excessive and reflects their privileged lifestyle.

The lack of a full stop mirrors the idea of viewing an incomplete picture.

Starting this stanza in the same way as the last encourages the reader to make a direct comparison. This makes the shift to a war-torn street more jarring — it jolts the reader.

Differences in language reinforce the divide shown. The simple adjectives in this stanza are a stark contrast to the complex ones in the previous stanza.

Children looking after children — shows how unnatural war is.

The repeated sibilant sounds create a more sinister tone than is found in the previous stanza.

Shooting the photo is likened to shooting a gun.

The word "first" implies that the bombing is expected and that more will follow.

First full stop at the end of a stanza. The silent pause after the 'shot' becomes haunting.

The darkness the girl has to face is too great for someone so young.

The child and baby are dehumanised — the baby becomes a "burden" and the child obeys her survival instinct.

The reader is never told exactly what happened, just like the public in the poem.

Heaven and Hell are the ultimate opposites. Saying hell is "like" heaven is shocking and provokes a response from the reader.

Speaker distances themselves from the publishers by using the third-person pronoun.

One interpretation of this is that it's easy to slip from heaven into hell. It might be that the speaker is suggesting that unless society becomes less ignorant to the truth, they are dooming their own souls.

Hints that the girl and baby died. Graphic final image that will stay in the reader's mind.

There isn't a 'tidy' ending to the poem. The ending is ambiguous and open to many interpretations — just like the photos it describes.

The reader can now see behind this positive 'frame' — like the speaker, they now know the truth.

The reassurance of the frame is flexible
– you can think that just outside it
people eat, sleep, love normally
while I seek out the tragic, the absurd,
5   to make a subject.
Or if the picture's such as lifts the heart
the firmness of the edges can convince you
this is how things are

– as when at Ascot once
10   I took a pair of peach, sun-gilded girls
rolling, silk-crumpled, on the grass
in champagne giggles

– as last week, when I followed a small girl
staggering down some devastated street,
15   hip thrust out under a baby's weight.
She saw me seeing her; my finger pressed.

At the corner, the first bomb of the morning
shattered the stones.
Instinct prevailing, she dropped her burden
20   and, mouth too small for her dark scream,
began to run...

The picture showed the little mother
the almost-smile. Their caption read
'Even in hell the human spirit
25   triumphs over all.'
But hell, like heaven, is untidy,
its boundaries
arbitrary as a blood stain on a wall.

POEM DICTIONARY
absurd — senseless, ridiculous
Ascot — a racecourse in Berkshire, England
gilded — covered in a layer of gold
arbitrary — random, decided for no particular reason

Carole Satyamurti

Carole Satyamurti is a poet, translator and sociologist. She often writes about painful subjects in her poetry. Her poem 'War Photographer' was written in 1987 — a time when several major conflicts were ongoing.

You've got to know what the poem's about

1) The speaker says that when people see a tragic image, they often assume it has been sought out. However, if it's a pleasant image, people will think it's the norm and an accurate portrayal of real life.

2) Two photos are described — one of two wealthy women at the races and another of a little girl in a war-torn street carrying a baby. It's revealed that after the speaker took the second photo, a bomb went off and the terrified girl ran for her life, abandoning the baby she was looking after.

3) The final stanza reveals that the second photograph didn't tell the whole story when it was published. The speaker distances themselves from how it has been presented to the public.

Learn about the form, structure and language

1) **FORM** — The poem is written in free verse (it has no formal rhyme scheme or rhythm). This reveals the speaker's thoughts in a natural style and mirrors their interest in the 'truth' — their words aren't 'dressed up' in rhyme. The varying stanza and line lengths also reflect the idea of frames having flexibility.

2) **STRUCTURE** — The poem has a cyclical structure: it begins and ends by considering how 'frames' and "boundaries" are changeable. However, while they start off as a source of "reassurance", these frames quickly become menacing as they show how easy it is to ignore suffering.

3) **CONTRASTS** — The poet uses contrasts to highlight parallels and differences. Luxurious language and imagery presents the Ascot girls as beautiful and "sun-gilded", whereas the girl in the war zone is "small" and "staggering". The settings of comfortable "grass" and a "devastated street" reinforce this divide. These contrasts connect the girls while emphasising the huge difference in their experiences.

4) **EMOTIVE LANGUAGE** — The poem contains powerful, emotive descriptions of the war zone. The horror of this human suffering makes the reader uncomfortable and forces them to confront the truth.

5) **POSITIVE LANGUAGE** — Pleasant language is used to describe what society believes is the norm. However, the positive language in the final stanza is ironic, as the reader knows what really happened.

Remember the feelings and attitudes in the poem

1) **TRUTH** — The speaker wants society to understand the tragic truth behind what they see.

2) **IGNORANCE** — Society tends to focus on the positive side of things as opposed to how they really are.

3) **DETACHMENT** — The speaker is trapped behind their camera and is unable to help the little girl. All they can do is follow, watch from a distance and record the events as they unfold.

Go a step further and give a personal response

Have a go at answering these questions to help you come up with your own ideas about the poem:

Q1.   How do you think the speaker feels about "how things are" (line 8)?

Q2.   What effect does the phrase "She saw me seeing her" (line 16) have?

Q3.   Why do you think the poet chose to make both of the memories about girls?

Conflict in wartime, reality of conflict, loss and suffering...

The senselessness of war could be compared with the soldier's realisation in 'The Man He Killed'. 'Belfast Confetti' and 'What Were They Like?' show some of the other difficulties in talking about war.

Belfast Confetti

Starts in the middle of the action — disorientates the reader.

These bits of scrap metal were used as missiles by nationalists during riots in Belfast and earned the name 'Belfast confetti'.

The phrase is broken up as though it too has exploded. This disorientates the reader.

Reflects the speaker's fear as well as the sound of gunfire.

A colon is a punctuation mark and a part of the intestines. This implies corpses are in the streets.

Comparing an area the speaker knows well to a labyrinth emphasises their confusion. May be a reference to the Greek myth of Theseus and the Minotaur, or to Maze Prison outside Belfast, which held paramilitary prisoners during the Troubles.

Frustrated with helplessness and inability to get to safety.

The lack of a comma after "Suddenly" shows how fast everything happened — it's as though there's no time to pause for breath.

Riots were sometimes started to lure security services into the blast radius of a bomb.

Metaphor conveys the alarm and intense sound of the explosion. It also creates a visual image of debris falling all around.

"fount" can mean 'font' (a style that text can be written in). This meaning, along with the phrase "broken type", suggests that words are not able to accurately describe the carnage.

Both a visual representation of the explosion and how the police might mark it on a map.

Dashes and ellipsis give images of bullets firing.

Harsh 'k' and 'eh' sounds imply violence, cracking and breaking.

Assonant 'o' sounds add to the claustrophobic feeling of being trapped.

Street names situate the poem geographically, but also in the context of a wider conflict.

Implies rigid control by the police.

The speaker can't concentrate or gather their thoughts — they simply list what can be seen.

These may be questions the speaker is being asked or they could be questions they ask themselves. The chaos can be seen to have stripped them of their identity. The lack of answers also indicates that the speaker can't think straight.

Lines end abruptly. This shows the lack of progress in the speaker's attempt to flee, and in the resolution of the conflict between nationalists and unionists.

Suddenly as the riot squad moved in, it was raining exclamation marks,
Nuts, bolts, nails, car-keys. A fount of broken type. And the explosion.
Itself - an asterisk on the map. This hyphenated line, a burst of rapid fire…
I was trying to complete a sentence in my head but it kept stuttering,
5 All the alleyways and side streets blocked with stops and colons.

I know this labyrinth so well - Balaclava, Raglan, Inkerman, Odessa Street -
Why can't I escape? Every move is punctuated. Crimea Street. Dead end again.
A Saracen, Kremlin-2 mesh. Makrolon face-shields. Walkie-talkies. What is
My name? Where am I coming from? Where am I going? A fusillade of question-marks.

Context — The Troubles
This poem was written in 1990, when the Troubles (1968-1998) were still ongoing. Irish nationalists wanted the whole of Ireland to become an independent republic, while unionists wanted Northern Ireland to remain part of the United Kingdom. British soldiers had become a frequent presence on the streets of Northern Ireland, and were often targeted by protesters who resented the British rule they represented.

POEM DICTIONARY
fount — an alternative spelling of 'font', or a fountain
type — printed letters and characters
Balaclava, Raglan, Inkerman, Odessa Street, Crimea Street — streets in Belfast named after events and leaders from the Crimean War
Saracen — an armoured army vehicle
Kremlin-2 mesh — anti-rocket netting fitted to tanks
Makrolon — a type of plastic
fusillade — a series of shots fired very quickly

Ciaran Carson

Ciaran Carson was born in Belfast in 1948. This poem was written in 1990 during the Troubles. This was a 30-year conflict which saw lots of violence take place between Irish nationalists and unionists.

You've got to know what the poem's about

1) The speaker explains that the <u>riot police</u> had just arrived when a <u>bomb went off</u> in Belfast.

2) They describe the blast in a very figurative way and explain how all of their attempts to <u>escape</u> amidst the <u>panic</u> fail because every path is <u>blocked</u>.

3) The poem ends in a state of <u>fear</u> and <u>confusion</u> as the speaker <u>struggles to make sense</u> of the situation.

Learn about the form, structure and language

1) **FORM** — Irregular line lengths, incomplete sentences, caesurae and enjambment all give the poem a <u>fragmented</u> feel, and reflect how the speaker is <u>struggling</u> to <u>think clearly</u>. The lines appear <u>broken</u>, mimicking how the speaker repeatedly reaches dead ends as they attempt to <u>flee</u> the violence.

2) **STRUCTURE** — The poem starts *in medias res* (in the <u>middle</u> of the action) and does not reach any real conclusion. This imitates the speakers's <u>confused memories</u> of the event. The poem has two stanzas: the first is in the past tense and the second is in the present tense. This <u>shift</u> creates a sense of <u>immediacy</u> and shows that the <u>confusion</u> is still <u>ongoing</u> — the speaker can't come to terms with what they saw.

3) **LANGUAGE ABOUT DESTRUCTION** — <u>Imagery</u> of fragmentation, and the frequent use of violent verbs (e.g. "burst") and adjectives (e.g. "broken") all work to reinforce the impression of <u>devastation</u>.

4) **LANGUAGE ABOUT PUNCTUATION** — Punctuation usually shows <u>structure</u>, so by scattering punctuation words throughout the poem, the poet conveys a complete <u>loss of control</u>. Punctuation is almost described as a <u>weapon</u> (e.g. bullets become a "hyphenated line"), bringing <u>terror</u> instead of <u>order</u>.

5) **CHAOTIC LANGUAGE** — The use of unanswered questions <u>emphasises</u> the speaker's <u>confusion</u>. Lists of objects make them seem <u>overwhelmed</u>, as though they're surrounded by noise and <u>chaos</u>.

Remember the feelings and attitudes in the poem

1) **PANIC** — The poem describes a personal and <u>emotional reaction</u> to a bomb attack in Belfast. The speaker tries to explain their <u>terror</u> and <u>confusion</u>, but finds it nearly impossible to do so clearly.

2) **DISORIENTATION** — Physical violence and commotion <u>distress</u> and <u>bewilder</u> the speaker.

3) **BEING TRAPPED** — The speaker is <u>physically trapped</u> in blockaded streets. They also experience a <u>mental block</u> as they find it hard to understand what is happening and make sense of their surroundings.

Go a step further and give a personal response

Have a go at <u>answering</u> these <u>questions</u> to help you come up with <u>your own ideas</u> about the poem:

Q1.	Why do you think Carson chose the title he did? Do you think it's effective?
Q2.	Do you think the poem depicts the aftermath of an explosion effectively? Why?
Q3.	What does the use of the word "again" in line 7 suggest about how the speaker feels?
Q4.	What is the effect of naming technical equipment in the penultimate line?

Effects of conflict, individual experiences, fear...

You could compare the bomb incident in this poem with that in 'War Photographer'. You could also pair this poem with 'Exposure' — both present the horrors of conflict from a realistic, first-person perspective.

The Class Game

The speaker addresses the listener directly. This makes them seem defensive — as though they're responding to a comment.

The impersonal nature of "some" creates distance and a bitter, angry tone.

The short, simple 'a' sound in "an 'at" contrasts with the long 'ar' sound in "scarf" — this helps to emphasise the difference.

The speaker could "talk posh" if they wanted to, but they are happy as they are. By making it their choice, the speaker regains power.

Plays on the phrase 'to look down your nose at someone', meaning to be snobbish.

Repetition of the opening question emphasises the speaker's point and refocuses their argument.

Sarcastic tone makes the 'posh' goodbye seem insincere. Having "dear" on a line by itself makes it seem disjointed, as though it is too formal.

Use of a dialect word to describe their council house implies their pride in it.

Cute adjectives seem sarcastic and imply that the speaker finds the semi unimpressive and only superficially beautiful.

Language creates a playground atmosphere — suggests judging people on their class is immature.

The image of a physical label encourages readers to consider figurative class labels. Labelling people also dehumanises them.

Contrasting light and dark imagery provides a visual comparison of how differently society views the two classes.

Comical simile that mocks how posh people might feel when reading this poem with all its slang.

Exaggerated image of a stereotypically posh mannerism mocks the middle classes for aspiring to be aristocratic.

A usually friendly term is used aggressively. The exclamation mark adds intensity, revealing how angry the speaker really is.

The question the speaker has been building towards. The 'how' can be answered easily, but the 'why' cannot — there's no reason why the speaker's class should matter to anyone.

How can you tell what class I'm from?
I can talk posh like some
With an 'Olly in me mouth
Down me nose, wear an 'at not a scarf
5   With me second-hand clothes.
So why do you always wince when you hear
Me say 'Tara' to me 'Ma' instead of 'Bye Mummy
        dear'?
How can you tell what class I'm from?
'Cos we live in a corpy, not like some
10   In a pretty little semi, out Wirral way
And commute into Liverpool by train each day?
Or did I drop my unemployment card
Sitting on your patio (We have a yard)?
How can you tell what class I'm from?
15   Have I a label on me head, and another on me bum?
Or is it because my hands are stained with toil?
Instead of soft lily-white with perfume and oil?
Don't I crook me little finger when I drink me tea
Say toilet instead of bog when I want to pee?
20   Why do you care what class I'm from?
Does it stick in your gullet like a sour plum?
Well, mate! A cleaner is me mother
A docker is me brother
Bread pudding is wet nelly
25   And me stomach is me belly
And I'm proud of the class that I come from.

Presents their family members and background — shows their pride in where they come from.

Rather than ending by repeating their question again, the speaker realises how unimportant it is — how they feel is all that matters.

The speaker takes pride in their heritage by choosing the local name over the more formal, popular name.

POEM DICTIONARY
'Olly — can mean 'marble' in Liverpool slang
corpy — Liverpool slang term for a council house
semi — a semi-detached house
Wirral — a borough in Merseyside that is considered 'posh' by some.
toil — hard work, usually physical labour
gullet — the part of the throat that food passes through to reach the stomach
docker — someone who works in a port loading and unloading boats

Melvin's favourite class game was pretty shocking.

Mary Casey

This poem was published in 1979 in 'Voices', a magazine which strived to publish poems written by ordinary people instead of professional writers. It is based on Casey's own life and experiences in Liverpool.

You've got to know what the poem's about

1) The speaker asks someone of a higher social class how they can identify what class they are from.

2) They ask why they're being judged for not being posh and sarcastically compare social stereotypes.

3) The examples are mostly humorous, but repeated rhetorical questions reveal the speaker's frustration.

4) The speaker ultimately says that they are proud of who they are, regardless of what anyone else thinks.

Learn about the form, structure and language

1) **FORM** — The pronouns "I" and "you" are used to emphasise the division between the working and middle classes. The poem has an imperfect form — it's mostly written in rhyming couplets (which is a traditional form), but some are half rhymes. This reflects the speaker's belief that their informal language is important — they don't stick to formal conventions because they're proud of their own identity.

2) **STRUCTURE** — The poem can be seen to have a one-sided question and answer structure — the speaker asks rhetorical questions and responds to them with even more questions. After each repetition of "How can you tell what class I'm from?", the speaker asks about different elements of their identity. The final change to "I'm proud of the class that I come from" provides a clear conclusion to the poem.

3) **DIALECT** The poem contains Liverpudlian dialect, which gives the voice of the speaker authenticity and gives the reader a stronger sense of their character. This makes the poem more engaging.

4) **COLLOQUIAL LANGUAGE** — Working-class slang makes the poem sound like it would be spoken. This reinforces the speaker's pride in their class — they won't change their language to suit others. This language also creates a sense of familiarity, which encourages the reader to sympathise with the speaker.

5) **CONTRASTS** — Referring to the middle class as "you" and "some" contrasts with the more personal "I" and "we" that are used to describe the speaker and the working class — this emphasises the divide between the two social groups. However, pairing different words for the same thing (e.g. "patio" and "yard") shows how trivial this divide is. These contrasts also stop when the speaker describes their pride.

Remember the feelings and attitudes in the poem

1) JUDGEMENT — The speaker feels judged by others because they are from a working-class family.

2) FRUSTRATION — The speaker's frustration resonates with each rhetorical question that they ask.

3) PRIDE — Despite feeling judged, the speaker takes pride in their social identity and way of life.

Go a step further and give a personal response

Have a go at answering these questions to help you come up with your own ideas about the poem:

Q1.   Do you think the speaker wants an actual answer to any of their questions? Why / why not?

Q2.   What is significant about the image of the hands that are "soft lily-white"?

Q3.   What effect does the second-person pronoun "you" have on the reader?

KEY THEMES

Conflict in society, identity, anger...

Social conflict and identity are also explored in 'No Problem' and 'Half-caste'. The ignorance of society crops up in 'War Photographer' too, and misleading outward appearances also feature in 'Cousin Kate'.

Poppies

An ominous reminder that war kills individuals, so loss is personal.

Makes the reader think of an injured body.

Another image of being wounded. She is emotionally wounded and he might be wounded in war.

Caesurae reflect the mother's attempt to stay in control — she doesn't want to get carried away with her emotions.

"felt" suggests she speaks softly and aligns her with domesticity.

The mother's composure briefly disappears, as shown by the "melting" of her words.

Simile shows the world from the son's perspective — makes it sound exciting and full of precious experiences.

Doves are a symbol of peace but also of mourning.

Battle imagery makes her sound vulnerable.

A reminder of the risks her son faces.

Strong visual image of something small and beautiful in a vast space — represents her son.

Repetition emphasises the parallel between national and personal mourning and remembrance.

Suggests that she feels shut out from her son's life.

Domestic, motherly image — this may be the last time she can do this for her son.

Alliteration emphasises she's trying to be brave and not show emotion.

This reference to the sense of touch shows how the mother longs for the closeness she had with her son when he was small, and emphasises the distance between them now.

The "blackthorns" allude to Jesus, who wore a crown of thorns when he was crucified. This hints at the sacrifice the son may make.

The mother asserting her bravery here subverts the idea that it's only those who go off to war who are brave.

The son's excitement contrasts with his mother's sadness. However, "intoxicated" also hints at a lack of control — the son's giving up control of his life by joining the army.

Symbolises her son leaving.

Sewing imagery conveys her nervousness and physical feelings of anxiety.

Touch is important to the mother — the memorial is a solid object, unlike her wishes and memories.

Strong visual image hints at her wish for his safety.

Alliteration echoes the way she's straining to hear him.

Links leaving to join the army with leaving to go to school.

Three days before Armistice Sunday
and poppies had already been placed
on individual war graves. Before you left,
I pinned one onto your lapel, crimped petals,
5 spasms of paper red, disrupting a blockade
of yellow bias binding around your blazer.

Sellotape bandaged around my hand,
I rounded up as many white cat hairs
as I could, smoothed down your shirt's
10 upturned collar, steeled the softening
of my face. I wanted to graze my nose
across the tip of your nose, play at
being Eskimos like we did when
you were little. I resisted the impulse
15 to run my fingers through the gelled
blackthorns of your hair. All my words
flattened, rolled, turned into felt,
slowly melting. I was brave, as I walked
with you, to the front door, threw
20 it open, the world overflowing
like a treasure chest. A split second
and you were away, intoxicated.
After you'd gone I went into your bedroom,
released a song bird from its cage.
25 Later a single dove flew from the pear tree,
and this is where it has led me,
skirting the church yard walls, my stomach busy
making tucks, darts, pleats, hat-less, without
a winter coat or reinforcements of scarf, gloves.

30 On reaching the top of the hill I traced
the inscriptions on the war memorial,
leaned against it like a wishbone.
The dove pulled freely against the sky,
an ornamental stitch. I listened, hoping to hear
35 your playground voice catching on the wind.

POEM DICTIONARY

Armistice — an agreement to end fighting. The armistice signed at the end of World War One, along with the people who died in the conflict, are remembered in November each year.

bias binding — a strip of fabric sewn on to conceal rough edges or add decoration. It could indicate the son's rank or regiment here.

Jane Weir

Jane Weir is a writer and textile designer who grew up in Manchester and Italy, and has also lived in Belfast. 'Poppies' was one of a collection of 21st-century war poems commissioned in 2009 by Carol Ann Duffy.

You've got to know what the poem's about

1) A mother describes her son leaving home, seemingly to join the army.

2) The poem is about the mother's emotional reaction to her son leaving — she feels sad, lonely and scared for his safety.

3) She describes helping him smarten his uniform ready to leave. After he leaves, she goes to places that remind her of him, desperately trying to find any trace of him.

Learn about the form, structure and language

1) **FORM** — The first-person narrative means that the reader gets a strong impression of the mother's emotions. There is no regular rhyme or rhythm, which makes it sound like the speaker's thoughts and memories. Long sentences and enjambment give the impression that the speaker is absorbed in her own thoughts and memories, whilst caesurae show how she tries to hold her emotions together.

2) **STRUCTURE** — The poem is chronological, describing preparing for the son leaving, his departure and then what the mother does afterwards. However, the time frame is ambiguous — memories of the son's childhood are intermingled with memories of him leaving, and they're often not clearly distinguished.

3) **USE OF THE SENSES** — The mother's separation from her son is shown by the way she can't touch or hear him. She touches other things and listens for his voice "on the wind", but this can't replace her son.

4) **WAR IMAGERY** — Images of war and violence symbolise the son's new identity and the danger he's in. References to "Armistice Sunday" and the "war memorial" make the reader question whether he is alive.

5) **DOMESTIC IMAGERY** — The images of war are mixed with poignant images of home and family life.

Remember the feelings and attitudes in the poem

1) **LOSS** — The mother acts as if she's lost her son — she is struggling to move on and accept the changes. There are hints that the son may even be dead. References to the son starting school allude to a different kind of loss that the mother has previously experienced.

2) **FEAR** — The mother is anxious and fearful for her son's safety. Her anxiety has a physical effect on her. The poem focuses on the bravery and restraint of the people left behind when their loved ones go to war.

3) **FREEDOM** — The poem shows the contrasting perspectives between the loss the mother feels and the freedom and excitement her son experiences.

Go a step further and give a personal response

Have a go at answering these questions to help you come up with your own ideas about the poem:

Q1.   Is this a poem about war or a poem about family? Explain your answer.
Q2.   What impression do you get of the mother through the things that she does?
Q3.   Do you think the son is still alive? What clues does the poem give you?
Q4.   How do you think the title relates to the poem?

Effects of conflict, memory, loss and suffering...

Effects of conflict are covered in several poems, including 'Exposure'. You could also compare this poem with family identity in 'Catrin', memory in the extract from 'The Prelude' or loss in 'What Were They Like?'.

Section One — The Poems

No Problem

The title is revealed to be ironic as this very first line tells the reader that there is, in fact, a problem.

Suggests that stereotypes are preventing them from fulfilling their real purpose. Connotations of slavery are attached to "branded" — this links the speaker's individual experience to a much wider issue.

Non-standard grammar helps to create an authentic voice — this makes the plea more heartfelt.

Repetition shows the speaker's burning desire to show what they can really do. The use of "can" implies there's potential for change to happen.

Defiance — the speaker will always resist the constraints society tries to place on them.

Compares effects of racism to a long-term disease. Emphasises how it can take its toll on someone.

Shift from "I" to "Black" as the speaker includes everyone who has been similarly oppressed. This highlights how the racial issues in the poem are widespread.

The speaker demands change. "Mother country" could be seen as affectionate (the speaker sees England as their home) or as a subtle reference to ancestral 'motherlands', which were colonised.

The repeated plosive 'b' sound mimics physical blows landing. Shows the strength of the speaker as they carry the weight of this responsibility even though it is not theirs to bear.

Sibilance creates a sinister hissing sound, which is often used to show contempt. It's ambiguous whether adults are using childish taunts or whether children are mimicking racist language.

Each time this refrain is repeated, the speaker goes on to reveal another aspect of the real problem — white society's refusal to treat the speaker as an equal.

Alludes to the 'criminal' stereotype that black people face — they are expected to be 'on the run' from police.

Phonetic spelling of "yu" accentuates the internal rhyme, and makes the speaker's voice seem happier and more lyrical when describing their abilities.

Pigeonholing is putting complex things into small, restrictive categories. This shows injustice — the speaker is kind, but treated harshly.

Double positive stresses the sincerity of the speaker.

To have a 'chip on your shoulder' means to be upset or angry because you feel that you've been treated unfairly. The speaker's refusal to become hateful towards their oppressors can be seen as a form of moral defiance.

Parodies a typical excuse used to justify saying racially problematic things. Reducing the phrase to a joke exposes how weak an excuse it is.

The poem's only full stop comes at the end. This suggests that the speaker feels passionately about the issue and wanted to get all their thoughts out at once. It also places emphasis on "white" being the last word.

I am not de problem
But I bear de brunt
Of silly playground taunts
An racist stunts,
5   I am not de problem
I am born academic
But dey got me on de run
Now I am branded athletic
I am not de problem
10   If yu give I a chance
I can teach yu of Timbuktu
I can do more dan dance,
I am not de problem
I greet yu wid a smile
15   Yu put me in a pigeon hole
But I am versatile

These conditions may affect me
As I get older,
An I am positively sure
20   I have no chips on me shoulders,
Black is not de problem
Mother country get it right
An juss fe de record,
Sum of me best friends are white.

Benjamin Zephaniah

Benjamin Zephaniah was born in Birmingham in 1958. His parents are Caribbean, and his Jamaican heritage often influences his poetry — as it does in this poem about racism, which was published in 1996.

You've got to know what the poem's about

1) The speaker talks about their <u>experiences</u> of <u>racial stereotyping</u> in <u>England</u>.

2) For example, they are <u>naturally clever</u>, but were <u>expected</u> to be <u>sporty</u> instead.

3) They say that there's <u>more</u> to them than people think — they won't let these <u>prejudices restrict</u> them.

4) Looking ahead, they understand that racism will continue to affect them, but they <u>call for change</u>.

Learn about the form, structure and language

1) **FORM** — The use of <u>personal pronouns</u> throughout the poem highlights how this is a <u>real story</u> and encourages the reader to <u>care</u> about the speaker. The poem has a <u>regular ABCB rhyme scheme</u> and looks at a new part of the problem every four lines. While it would probably have been more <u>conventional</u> to use <u>quatrains</u> (stanzas of four lines), the decision to use two stanzas of different lengths reflects the speaker's message that they are more than simply what is expected of them.

2) **STRUCTURE** — The poem is split into two parts. The first stanza describes how the speaker has been affected by <u>racist stereotypes</u>. In the second stanza, they look to the <u>future</u> and hope for change.

3) **PHONETIC CARIBBEAN ENGLISH** — The words are spelt the way they sound when <u>spoken</u> aloud — this makes the speaker's voice seem <u>authentic</u> and reveals how proud they are of their <u>cultural heritage</u>. Using a voice which is stereotyped against to try and fight stereotypes shows their <u>strength</u> and <u>defiance</u>.

4) **LANGUAGE OF VICTIMISATION** — By presenting themselves as a <u>victim</u> of racism, the speaker creates a <u>sympathetic response</u> and makes the reader <u>question</u> the impact of their own stereotyping.

5) **LANGUAGE OF DEFIANCE** — The speaker repeatedly demonstrates how they are more <u>complex</u> than people expect them to be, and their <u>demand</u> for change emphasises their <u>determination</u> and <u>spirit</u>.

Remember the feelings and attitudes in the poem

1) **OPPRESSION** — The speaker reveals the <u>racism</u> and <u>adversity</u> they have faced. Due to the colour of their skin, they battled <u>abuse</u> and additional <u>limitations</u> while they were growing up.

2) **HOPE** — Despite past <u>prejudice</u>, and the likelihood of more in the future, the speaker remains <u>hopeful</u>. They know that they are <u>not the problem</u> and understand that the <u>potential for change</u> exists — people can still "get it right" and stop harmful racial stereotyping.

Go a step further and give a personal response

Have a go at <u>answering</u> these <u>questions</u> to help you come up with <u>your own ideas</u> about the poem:

Q1.   Do you think the speaker is happy living in their "Mother country"? Why / why not?

Q2.   How effective do you think the speaker's request for social change is?

Q3.   How do you think Zephaniah wanted to make different readers feel?

Conflict in society, identity, individual experiences...

KEY THEMES

Consider how the speakers in this poem, 'Half-caste' and 'The Class Game' stand up for their different cultural identities. You could also take a look at the sense of lost heritage in 'What Were They Like?'.

What Were They Like?

Numbering the questions suggests this was a planned interaction.

An almost magical image — creates a sense of wonder and mystery.

All of the questions are in the past tense — their way of life is clearly over now.

The formality of the response suggests some kind of hierarchy between the speakers, but their relationship is ambiguous.

Answers are cautious and uncertain — suggests that the information is lost or that the speaker doesn't want to say the wrong thing.

This blunt, shocking phrase contrasts with what's come before, highlighting how this is a brutal and bleak way of tracking the passage of time.

The meaning of bone has changed from line 6, where it was used for ornaments, to here, where the bones are the burnt bodies of the bombed.

Reminders of their tranquil lives are juxtaposed with images of war — this makes the violence seem more barbaric.

The shocking violence of these two lines shatters the peace of the previous six lines.

Shows their respect for nature and the peacefulness of the Vietnamese lifestyle.

Portrays the Vietnamese people as modest and gentle.

Refers to the figurative hardening of hearts caused by the inhumanity of war. Contrasts with the "lanterns of stone" on line 2.

Harsh alliteration emphasises the horror of the napalm bombing which burnt everything in its path — the plosive sounds suggest the speaker is suppressing anger.

Repetition reinforces the theme of remembrance.

The once still, peaceful water of the paddies is now compared to a broken mirror — this evokes the superstition of having bad luck after breaking a mirror.

Simile suggests a soft and gentle beauty.

1) Did the people of Viet Nam
   use lanterns of stone?
2) Did they hold ceremonies
   to reverence the opening of buds?
5 3) Were they inclined to quiet laughter?
4) Did they use bone and ivory,
   jade and silver, for ornament?
5) Had they an epic poem?
6) Did they distinguish between speech and singing?

10 1) Sir, their light hearts turned to stone.
    It is not remembered whether in gardens
    stone lanterns illumined pleasant ways.
2) Perhaps they gathered once to delight in blossom,
   but after their children were killed
15 there were no more buds.
3) Sir, laughter is bitter to the burned mouth.
4) A dream ago, perhaps. Ornament is for joy.
   All the bones were charred.
5) It is not remembered. Remember,
20 most were peasants; their life
   was in rice and bamboo.
   When peaceful clouds were reflected in the paddies
   and the water buffalo stepped surely along terraces,
   maybe fathers told their sons old tales.
25 When bombs smashed those mirrors
   there was time only to scream.
6) There is an echo yet
   of their speech which was like a song.
   It was reported that their singing resembled
30 the flight of moths in moonlight.
   Who can say? It is silent now.

The poem ends with a rhetorical question. They haven't really answered anything, but instead have raised more questions.

Their culture has been lost forever. The silence following this final statement is profoundly moving in comparison to all the wonderful noises of the past.

Context — The Vietnam War

The Vietnam War (1955-1975), was a conflict between North and South Vietnam. The US supported the South, but eventually withdrew and North Vietnam won. Although considered a humiliating defeat, the US still inflicted lots of damage on the Vietnamese people. Many were against the US involvement in Vietnam and publicly protested. Levertov's poem was written in the middle of this conflict and imagines a hypothetical future set after the war.

POEM DICTIONARY
ivory — a hard, white material that makes up animal tusks
jade — a hard, green-coloured type of stone
reverence — to show great respect and admiration
epic poem — a long poem, usually about important
           events in a culture's history
illumined — illuminated, lit up, brightened
charred — burnt until the outside turned black
paddies — fields that rice can be grown in

Denise Levertov

Denise Levertov was born in England, but moved to New York in 1948. She eventually became an American citizen, but strongly opposed the USA's involvement in the Vietnam War, as this 1967 poem demonstrates.

You've got to know what the poem's about

1) An individual asks a series of <u>questions</u> about the people of Vietnam and their culture, including their behaviour, art and language.

2) A second individual <u>answers</u> each question. It becomes apparent that Vietnam as it was known (a peaceful and happy country) no longer exists — it has been <u>utterly destroyed</u> by war.

3) The second individual answers the questions <u>formally</u>, but uses <u>vivid</u> and <u>graphic descriptions</u>. Talking about the <u>innocent beauty</u> Vietnam has lost seems to prompt an <u>emotional response</u> in them.

Learn about the form, structure and language

1) **FORM** — The <u>question and answer</u> form is <u>unusual</u> — it's not immediately recognisable as <u>free verse</u> poetry, much like how the poem's Vietnam is no longer identifiable. <u>Questions</u> and <u>caesurae</u> create natural <u>pauses</u> — these become poignant and touching in the context, and create a deep sense of loss.

2) **STRUCTURE** — The poem can be read from top to bottom or by reading each question and answer in turn. The <u>ambiguity</u> of how best to approach the poem mirrors the <u>discomfort</u> and <u>unease</u> that it conveys. The final answers are longer, which makes the <u>closing silence</u> more affecting and profound.

3) **PEACEFUL IMAGERY** — The poem is full of <u>idyllic images</u> of <u>nature</u> and rural farm life that create a sense of <u>calm</u>. This <u>contrasts</u> with the <u>destruction</u> caused by war and makes what happened to the poem's Vietnam seem even more appalling by comparison. The peaceful imagery becomes <u>tinged with sadness</u>.

4) **LANGUAGE OF DEVASTATION** — The terrible consequences of <u>warfare</u> are described in <u>vivid detail</u>. This <u>shocks</u> the reader and emphasises the <u>horror</u> of Vietnam having been <u>destroyed forever</u>.

5) **FORMAL TONE** — While the identity of the responding individual is <u>ambiguous</u>, their <u>respectful tone</u> can be <u>interpreted</u> as insincere and sarcastic — like they are <u>repressing</u> their <u>true feelings</u> about the war.

Remember the feelings and attitudes in the poem

1) **LOSS** — The loss of the Vietnamese people is emphasised through the <u>past tense</u> and phrases such as "A dream ago", which tell the reader that it <u>no longer exists</u>.

2) **SORROW** — The loss of innocent life and beauty is a source of great <u>sadness</u>, <u>anger</u> and <u>pain</u>. A <u>detailed picture</u> of Vietnam is painted in the reader's mind, before telling them that it is no more.

3) **DOUBT** — Phrases like "Perhaps" and "It was reported" create a sense of uncertainty, suggesting that for some aspects of Vietnamese culture, <u>no reliable information</u> remains.

Go a step further and give a personal response

Have a go at <u>answering</u> these <u>questions</u> to help you come up with <u>your own ideas</u> about the poem:

Q1. What sort of people do you think the two individuals could be? Explain your answer.

Q2. Why do you think the poet lists the four ornamental materials that she does?

Q3. What effect does the phrase "A dream ago, perhaps" (line 17) have on the reader?

Q4. How do you think the first speaker might respond after hearing the answers?

Conflict in wartime, effects of conflict, loss and suffering...

The shift from happiness to sorrow in this poem can be compared to that in 'War Photographer'. Loss on a large scale is also a theme in 'The Destruction of Sennacherib', and 'Poppies' looks at a personal loss.

Practice Questions

Congratulations, you've read all fifteen poems. Now it's time to check what you know — these handy questions cover all the poems you've just read, helping you to check you're getting to grips with each one.

A Poison Tree

1) Briefly explain what you think the poem is about.

2) Why do you think we are given so little information about the "foe"?

3) Why do you think Blake chose to use a tree as a metaphor for the speaker's anger?

The Destruction of Sennacherib

1) Briefly summarise what happens in the poem.

2) What mood is Byron trying to create in the poem? How does he achieve this?

3) Give an example of alliteration in the poem. What is the effect of this?

Extract from 'The Prelude'

1) What do you think Wordsworth is saying about man's relationship with nature?

2) How do the speaker's feelings change over the course of the extract?

3) Give an example of personification of the mountain. What is the effect of this?

The Man He Killed

1) How do the speaker's opinions change over the course of the poem?

2) Why do you think Hardy chose to write the poem using matter-of-fact language?

3) What is the effect of the caesurae in the poem?

Cousin Kate

1) Briefly explain how the speaker's relationship with the lord changed.

2) How does the tone of the poem change in the final stanza?

3) Find an example of a simile in the poem. What is its effect?

Practice Questions

Half-caste

1) What do you think the overall message of the poem is?

2) Do you think that 'Half-caste' is an angry poem? Explain your answer.

3) What is the effect of repetition in the poem?

Exposure

1) What do you think the poem's overall message is?

2) Does the tone of the poem change at all? Why do you think this is?

3) Give an example of a half-rhyme in the poem. What effect does it have?

The Charge of the Light Brigade

1) Write a brief summary of what happens in each stanza of the poem.

2) How does the speaker feel about the actions of the Light Brigade? How can you tell?

3) Find some examples of repetition in the poem. What is its effect?

Catrin

1) Briefly describe how the speaker feels about her daughter.

2) What is the effect of mentioning two different periods of time in the poem?

3) Find some examples of enjambment in the poem. What effect do they have?

War Photographer

1) What do you think the overall message of the poem is?

2) How does the mood change throughout the poem?

3) What do you think happened to the little girl? Explain your answer.

Practice Questions

Belfast Confetti

1) Briefly describe what happens in the poem.

2) How would you describe the speaker's relationship with Belfast?

3) How are words related to punctuation used to show the speaker's confusion?

The Class Game

1) What is the speaker's overall message in the poem?

2) Does the tone of the poem change at all? Why do you think this?

3) Find a simile in the poem and explain why it has been used.

Poppies

1) Briefly explain what happens in the poem.

2) What would you say is the overriding emotion in the poem? Explain your answer.

3) Why do you think there are so many references to the mother touching things?

No Problem

1) Briefly describe the issues that are explored in the poem.

2) What are the main feelings of the speaker in the poem? Do these feelings change at any point?

3) How important do you think the speaker's voice is in the poem? Explain your answer.

What Were They Like?

1) What is the effect of the questions and answers that are used in the poem?

2) How does the poem convey a sense of loss?

3) How do you think Levertov wanted to make people feel when they read the poem?

Practice Questions

Everyone loves exams, so this page is a real treat — it's jam-packed full of tasty exam-style questions. If you're one of those strange people who doesn't like exams, give some of them a go anyway — the more time you spend with these poems, the easier you'll find the real exam. Don't forget to write a plan before you start.

Exam-style Questions

1) Compare the way poets present ideas about attachment in 'Poppies' and one other poem from 'Conflict'.

2) Compare how the speakers' feelings towards society are presented in 'War Photographer' and one other poem from 'Conflict'.

3) Explore the ways in which anger is presented in 'Half-caste' and one other poem from 'Conflict'.

4) Compare the way in which chaos is conveyed in 'Belfast Confetti' and one other poem from 'Conflict'.

5) 'When people are in conflict, power is ultimately pointless.'

   Using this quotation as a starting point, write about the theme of power in 'The Destruction of Sennacherib' and one other poem from 'Conflict'.

   Remember to comment on how the poems are written.

Conflict in Wartime

Military conflict is a common theme in these poems — you didn't think this was going to be cheery, did you?

> 1) Some poets choose to write about <u>entire armies</u> and <u>battles</u> in their poems.
>
> 2) Other poets focus their writing on how war affects <u>individual people</u>.

War poetry can describe large-scale conflict...

The Destruction of Sennacherib (Pages 4-5)

1) The soldiers are described in <u>general</u> terms, such as "the sleepers" and "cohorts" — this implies that there are <u>so many</u> of them that they've become <u>one</u> large identical <u>group</u>. The simile of the "sheen of their spears" being "like stars" emphasises the incredibly <u>large number</u> of soldiers.

2) Similarly, the <u>stillness</u> at the end of the poem is shown through a description of the soldiers' <u>equipment</u> rather than the <u>dead soldiers</u>. The speaker presents the <u>bigger picture</u>, using the "silent" tents, "unlifted" lances and "unblown" trumpets to show the <u>scale</u> of their <u>defeat</u>.

The Charge of the Light Brigade (Pages 16-17)

1) The soldiers are not presented as <u>individuals</u> — they are always referred to as the "<u>six hundred</u>". This shows the <u>large-scale loss</u> that the charge resulted in, as the phrases "<u>Not</u> the six hundred" and "<u>Left</u> of six hundred" imply that <u>very few</u> of the original number returned.

2) Tennyson shows the <u>horror</u> and <u>violence</u> of battle. He describes the soldiers as riding into the "<u>jaws of Death</u>" and the "<u>mouth of Hell</u>", which suggests that they had little chance of <u>survival</u>.

...as well as personal experiences

The Man He Killed (Pages 8-9)

1) By focusing on just two soldiers, the poem uses an <u>individual experience</u> to present war. The speaker says that he was "face to face" with the soldier when he "shot at him as he at me". This creates a sense of <u>intimacy</u> and places the two men on an <u>equal footing</u>. Hardy's speaker wonders if his "foe" was really a foe, or if he was a very similar <u>individual</u> instead ("just as I").

2) The <u>colloquial language</u> gives the poem a clear, <u>vivid voice</u>, making it seem like a more <u>personal</u> account to the reader. It also shows that the people involved in war are often <u>ordinary</u> individuals.

Belfast Confetti (Pages 22-23)

1) The poem takes place in a location the speaker knows "<u>so well</u>". This makes the situation feel more <u>personal</u> and <u>heightens</u> the speaker's <u>panic</u> when they find themselves <u>unable to recognise</u> the "<u>labyrinth</u>" that Belfast has become in the aftermath of the explosion.

2) The trio of <u>personal questions</u> at the end of the poem emphasises how <u>confused</u> and <u>afraid</u> the speaker feels — it is as though they have <u>lost their identity</u> entirely.

3) The list of streets named after events and leaders from the Crimean War connects the speaker's <u>individual experience</u> of the Troubles to a <u>wider conflict</u>.

Other poems are also about wartime conflict...

'Exposure' and 'What Were They Like?' also explore the effects of conflict on large groups of people, while 'Poppies' and 'War Photographer' show that even those who don't fight can be affected by conflict.

Conflict in Society

Conflict doesn't just happen during wartime — you should see me fighting for a bargain in the sales.

> 1) Conflicts can occur due to the <u>relationships</u> and <u>emotions</u> between two people.
>
> 2) They can also occur between different <u>groups</u> of people, often due to <u>racial</u> or <u>class</u> prejudice.

Conflict can be between individuals...

A Poison Tree (Pages 2-3)

1) The reader doesn't find out <u>what</u> the source of the <u>conflict</u> is between the narrator and their foe. By not revealing it, Blake makes the poem's message more <u>universal</u> — it could <u>apply</u> to anyone.

2) The speaker is "<u>angry</u>" with both <u>friend</u> and <u>foe</u>, but because they have a <u>better relationship</u> with their friend, they <u>communicate</u> their feelings and "end" the conflict. This suggests that it would be better for society to be more open about negative feelings, rather than letting them become increasingly <u>toxic</u>.

Catrin (Pages 18-19)

1) 'Catrin' presents the relationship between a mother and daughter. Conflict is shown to be a natural part of their relationship, which is "<u>tender</u>", but also a source of <u>tension</u> ("Still I am fighting / You off").

Mama pig wished her piglets had the same need for separation...

2) The "Red rope of love which we both / Fought over" implies that they are two individuals <u>pulling</u> in <u>different directions</u>. This 'pulling away' is both <u>literal</u> during the birth and <u>emotional</u> during the argument when the daughter is older. This highlights how <u>tense</u> emotional conflict can be.

...or between individuals and society

No Problem (Pages 28-29)

1) The speaker draws attention to a <u>problem in society</u> — they discuss how <u>racial stereotyping</u> can limit people's individuality and unfairly put them in a "<u>pigeon hole</u>".

2) They reveal that they are not the "problem" and suggest that the problem really lies with <u>society</u> as a whole. This makes the reader question if they have contributed to the issue.

3) There's a sense of <u>optimism</u> at the end of the poem — if people let go of <u>prejudice</u> and "get it right", there's the potential for racial conflict to be <u>resolved</u> in the future.

The Class Game (Pages 24-25)

1) The speaker <u>confronts</u> someone of a higher social class and <u>challenges</u> the <u>assumptions</u> they have about individuals from <u>working-class</u> backgrounds.

2) <u>Contrasting language</u> is used to emphasise the <u>divide</u> between these social classes, e.g. the speaker's hands are "<u>stained</u> with toil" in comparison to the "<u>lily-white</u>" hands of the middle-class person they address. This stark contrast makes the two social groups seem <u>further apart</u> than they <u>really are</u>.

3) Likewise, <u>class stereotypes</u> are <u>exaggerated</u> to show this divide, when in reality the distinctions between the two are often <u>insignificant</u> (e.g. "yard" and "patio" are <u>almost synonyms</u>).

OTHER POEMS

You could also write about 'Cousin Kate'...

In 'Cousin Kate', conflict is explored on a personal level (there's conflict between the speaker and both Kate and the lord) as well as a societal one (the speaker is shunned by society for being "unclean").

Effects of Conflict

Death, death and more death — that's the gist of it, but thankfully the poets are a bit more creative than that.

> 1) Conflict causes <u>injury</u> (both physical and psychological) and <u>death</u>.
> 2) Even people <u>not</u> directly involved in the <u>conflict</u> can be <u>affected</u> by it.

Conflict affects those who fight...

The Destruction of Sennacherib (Pages 4-5)

1) The Assyrian army is <u>completely destroyed</u> — it's "blown" away like "leaves". While this is a <u>gentle simile</u> that implies the army was <u>peacefully defeated</u>, it still refers to a <u>massive loss of life</u>.

2) The graphic description of the horse's death reflects the <u>horror</u> and <u>suffering</u> of war. Likening "the <u>foam of his gasping</u>" to "the spray of the rock-beating surf" creates a violent image of the sea that contrasts with the earlier, more calming image of the "<u>blue wave</u>" rolling.

3) The final stanza shows the <u>pain</u> that war can cause. The soldier's widows are described as "loud in their wail", creating a <u>powerful</u> image of <u>despair</u>.

The Charge of the Light Brigade (Pages 16-17)

1) <u>Death</u> is the ultimate result of battle for many of the soldiers. The <u>repetition</u> of phrases such as "<u>Storm'd at with shot and shell</u>" and the line "<u>Some one had blunder'd</u>" creates an <u>ominous</u> mood and suggests that many of the soldiers will <u>die</u>.

2) The speaker focuses on the <u>extensive</u> loss of life in the charge — each stanza <u>ends</u> with a reference to the "<u>six hundred</u>" to remind the reader of the <u>huge human cost</u> involved.

3) The poem also shows how war can inspire great <u>bravery</u> and <u>sacrifice</u>. The soldiers do their <u>duty</u> even though they believe they are probably going to <u>die</u> in the process.

...as well as those who don't

Poppies (Pages 26-27)

1) 'Poppies' focuses on the <u>pain</u> and <u>distress</u> experienced by a <u>mother</u> whose son has joined the army. Even <u>before</u> he goes, the mother feels <u>detached</u> from her son — the "gelled / <u>blackthorns</u>" of his hair stop her running her fingers through it. This emotional distance <u>foreshadows</u> their physical <u>separation</u>.

2) After the son leaves, the mother is <u>anxious</u> and <u>restless</u>. Her <u>fear</u> for his safety is revealed in <u>physical symptoms</u> — she describes her <u>stomach</u> as "<u>busy</u> / making tucks, darts, pleats".

What Were They Like? (Pages 30-31)

1) Levertov examines how conflict can have effects <u>long after</u> it has <u>ended</u>. The poem's two speakers try to <u>connect</u> with Vietnam's <u>past</u>, but there is a sense of doubt because many of the answers are "<u>not remembered</u>". This highlights a tragic effect of conflict — the loss of a <u>rich culture</u> and <u>history</u>.

2) While there's a sense of uncertainty surrounding the previously peaceful way of life, the answers (e.g. "all the bones were charred") are <u>clearer</u> about the <u>brutal effects</u> of war. The <u>graphic</u>, <u>explicit</u> and <u>shocking</u> descriptions overshadow the past and highlight how only the <u>devastation</u> is certain now.

Other poems also consider the effects of conflict...

'Exposure' and 'Belfast Confetti' both show how conflict can also cause panic, fear and hopelessness. In contrast, 'War Photographer' explores how society is keen to avoid the effects of conflict altogether.

Reality of Conflict

These poems explain what it's really like to be directly involved in conflict (spoiler alert — it's not fun).

> 1) Poems set in the heat of the battle create <u>vivid pictures</u> of the sights, sounds and emotions.
>
> 2) Poems set after battles are more <u>detached</u>, but still confront the reader with the <u>horrors</u> of war.

The horror of conflict can be described as it happens...

Exposure (Pages 14-15)

1) <u>Bleak imagery</u> is used to convey the men's <u>pain</u> — for example, the description of the frost as "<u>puckering foreheads crisp</u>" compels the reader to imagine their <u>flesh freezing</u>. Comparing the noise of the wind to the "<u>twitching agonies</u> of men" creates a <u>vivid</u> picture of wounded soldiers.

2) The reality of war leaves no room for <u>patriotism</u> or <u>heroism</u> — the men "<u>cringe</u> in holes" like <u>frightened animals</u>. <u>Rhetorical questions</u> ("What are we doing here?") emphasise the <u>pointlessness</u> of the suffering.

3) The <u>hopeless tone</u> of the poem suggests that the men believe they have <u>little chance</u> of <u>surviving</u>. They seem to have accepted that they will never see their <u>families</u> or <u>homes</u> again.

Belfast Confetti (Pages 22-23)

1) The <u>first-person voice</u> gives the reader a direct insight into the <u>distressed</u> thoughts of the speaker as they feel increasingly overwhelmed by their <u>perilous surroundings</u>.

2) Frequent <u>lists</u> are combined with <u>caesurae</u> and <u>enjambment</u> (e.g. "A Saracen, Kremlin-2 mesh. Makrolon face-shields. Walkie- / talkies"). This gives the poem a <u>fragmented</u> feel, mirroring the speaker's <u>panic</u> and <u>disjointed thoughts</u> as they keep finding themselves <u>blocked</u> in.

3) The feeling of being <u>attacked</u> is emphasised by how <u>punctuation</u> is compared to weapons in phrases such as "A / fusillade of question-marks" — <u>symbols</u> of <u>order</u> have become <u>dangerous</u> and <u>harmful</u>.

...or after the event

The Charge of the Light Brigade (Pages 16-17)

1) The poem creates a <u>noisy</u> and <u>frightening</u> picture of the battle using onomatopoeia ("<u>thunder'd</u>"), violent verbs ("<u>Flash'd</u>") and a relentless, <u>galloping rhythm</u>. This emphasises the men's <u>bravery</u> and <u>heroism</u>.

2) However, there's a <u>distance</u> between the speaker and the battlefield — the battle is recounted like a <u>story</u>, and the <u>chronological structure</u> helps impose <u>order</u> on the events.

War Photographer (Pages 20-21)

1) The photographer describes the bombing <u>one week after</u> it happened. This creates a sense of <u>distance</u> that reflects how the photographer distanced themselves from the "small girl".

2) The <u>horror</u> of the moment is captured like a <u>snapshot</u>, but the <u>ellipsis</u> at the end of the phrase "began to run<u>...</u>" hints that the <u>full reality</u> of conflict <u>cannot</u> be <u>captured effectively</u> — what happened to the girl next is left to the reader's imagination.

The reality of conflict is also important in Hardy's poem...

In 'The Man He Killed', the speaker explains how the reality of war is ironic because people who may have been friends in other circumstances try to kill each other — it highlights how tragic this reality is.

Identity

I don't know what this 'ity' is — it's usually cars, walls or my bank balance that I dent...

> 1) <u>Belonging</u> to a <u>family</u> is an important part of human identity.
>
> 2) People take <u>pride</u> in their <u>individual</u> identities.

The Ruffington family portrait was a fancy affair.

Family identity can be complicated

Catrin (Pages 18-19)

1) 'Catrin' is about a mother's <u>struggle</u> as she and her daughter forge identities <u>independent</u> of each other.

2) Clarke presents what is traditionally an idealised, loving relationship in a <u>realistic</u> and <u>honest</u> way. The metaphor of the <u>umbilical cord</u> as a "<u>tight</u> / Red rope of love" highlights their joined identities as well as the <u>tension</u> caused by the first <u>battle</u> for <u>separation</u> — the birth. The rope metaphor is repeated in the second stanza, where it now <u>restricts</u> the speaker, who feels it "<u>Tightening</u>" about her "life".

3) <u>Enjambment</u> in the phrase "our struggle to become / Separate." highlights the mother and daughter's desire to become <u>individuals</u>. The <u>caesura</u> after "<u>Separate.</u>" emphasises the strength of this desire.

Poppies (Pages 26-27)

1) The boy's identity as a <u>son</u> is clearly established in the poem — his mother smooths down his collar and mentions that they used to "<u>play</u> at / being <u>Eskimos</u>" when he was <u>younger</u>.

2) However, the son has a <u>new identity</u> as a soldier and his "blazer" is a <u>visual reminder</u> of this. The mother <u>moving</u> from his <u>bedroom</u> to the "<u>war memorial</u>" reflects this change, as the bedroom is a <u>symbol</u> of <u>family</u> identity, but the war memorial <u>symbolises</u> his <u>new</u> identity as a soldier.

3) The mother still <u>clings</u> to his identity as her <u>son</u> and the poem ends with her trying to hear his "<u>playground voice</u>" — he's still her <u>child</u> and she longs for him to <u>return</u> to her.

People often take pride in their personal identity

Half-caste (Pages 12-13)

1) The mixture of <u>Caribbean dialect</u> and <u>standard English</u> reflects the speaker's <u>mixed heritage</u>.

2) By using <u>exaggerated metaphors</u> like "half of mih eye", the speaker shows the <u>absurdity</u> of the term "half-caste". This implies that they don't <u>identify</u> with the term and consider it <u>offensive</u>.

3) Instead, they use examples of how <u>mixing</u> creates <u>beauty</u>, such as art, music and the weather (e.g. "when picasso / mix red an green"). This shows their <u>pride</u> in having a mixed background.

The Class Game (Pages 24-25)

1) The speaker uses <u>slang</u> (e.g. "bog" and "Tara") and <u>Liverpudlian dialect</u> (e.g. "corpy" and "wet nelly"). This shows that they identify as part of Liverpool's <u>working class</u> and are <u>proud</u> of their identity.

2) A <u>confrontational tone</u> and <u>rhetorical questions</u> ("How can you tell what class I'm from?") show the speaker's <u>frustration</u> with how people from other social classes <u>judge</u> them. However, the speaker ultimately realises that all that matters is how <u>they</u> feel, and their question becomes a confident <u>statement</u> in the final line — "I'm proud of the class that I come from."

National identity is also important in some of the poems...

The speaker in 'The Charge of the Light Brigade' believes that the men should be honoured as national heroes. In 'What Were They Like?', the speakers try to recover a national identity which has been lost.

Memory

They say an elephant never forgets, so whack your trunks on and you'll remember this theme forever...

> 1) Memories can be <u>powerful</u>, particularly memories of <u>personal experiences</u>.
>
> 2) Memories of <u>difficult events</u> can be <u>troubling</u>, <u>uncertain</u> or <u>lost</u> altogether.

Memories can be described vividly...

Poppies (Pages 26-27)

1) The mother <u>clings to memories</u> of her son throughout the poem. Memories from <u>different time frames</u> are <u>intermingled</u> throughout the poem — her son in his childhood and him leaving to join the army. This shows how she is <u>unable to move on</u> with her life now he is "gone" — she lives in the <u>past</u>.

2) <u>Memories</u> of her son's childhood, e.g. when they would "play at / being Eskimos", create a sense of <u>innocence</u> that becomes poignant when contrasted with images of "war graves" and the "memorial".

3) The mother's memories seem to have been <u>influenced</u> by her <u>emotions</u>. It's unlikely that she literally released "a song bird" in her son's bedroom, but the <u>powerful feeling</u> of losing her son has impressed this <u>symbolic image</u> in her mind so <u>vividly</u> that she sees it when she <u>remembers</u> the day he left.

Catrin (Pages 18-19)

1) The phrase "I can remember you" is <u>repeated</u> in the poem. This reinforces the importance of the speaker's memories as she reflects upon how her daughter's life has <u>shaped</u> her own.

2) <u>Sensory language</u> makes the mother's memories more <u>vivid</u>. Describing the hospital room as "hot" and "white" shows how she can still <u>feel</u> and <u>see</u> the events in her mind — the experience of remembering is made almost as real as the experience itself. The <u>intensity</u> of the memories help the mother to examine how little her feelings have changed, and helps the reader <u>visualise</u> the scene.

...but sometimes they can be less clear

The Man He Killed (Pages 8-9)

1) Instead of giving the reader a <u>dramatic</u> account of his <u>memory</u>, the speaker describes killing the man in a <u>controlled</u> manner. The memory is presented in <u>simple</u>, <u>monosyllabic</u> language ("I shot at him as he at me") — the reader doesn't seem to get an impression of how he was <u>feeling</u> at the time.

2) The third and fourth stanzas introduce <u>doubt</u> through <u>caesurae</u> and <u>end-stopping</u> ("he'd 'list, perhaps, / Off-hand like — just as I —"). The more he thinks about the memory, the less certain he becomes.

What Were They Like? (Pages 30-31)

1) In the poem, Vietnam has been so <u>destroyed</u> by war that no <u>memories</u> of the people or culture remain — "<u>It is not remembered</u>" if the Vietnamese people used "lanterns of stone" or had "an epic poem".

2) The line "maybe fathers told their sons old tales" implies that <u>memories</u> and <u>histories</u> were <u>passed down</u> from generation to generation. However, the only memories that are left relate to the <u>horrors</u> that took place. Emotive phrases, such as "their children were killed", "bones were charred" and "there was only time to scream", emphasise the <u>devastation</u> that has <u>replaced everything</u> that came before.

OTHER POEMS

'The Prelude' also features a powerful memory...

The speaker in the extract is deeply troubled by his memories of the mountain — personification presents the mountain as a powerful and intimidating presence that haunts the speaker's "dreams".

Nature

Ahh, nature — I'm thinking of a sunny spring morning filled with daffodils and ducklings. Sadly not...

1) Poets often use imagery associated with <u>nature</u> to present <u>conflict</u> and <u>death</u>.
2) <u>Nature</u> can also be presented as the <u>cause</u> of <u>conflict</u>.

Natural imagery can be used to describe conflict

A Poison Tree (Pages 2-3)

1) The speaker's <u>anger</u> is presented through the <u>extended metaphor</u> of a tree.
2) The metaphor shows how the speaker's anger naturally grows <u>out of control</u>. Using a metaphor associated with nature to describe someone's increasing feeling of anger ("my wrath did grow") <u>contrasts</u> with the <u>positive connotations</u> that are usually linked to the <u>natural world</u>.
3) The image of the '<u>poison apple</u>' is another example of how something <u>natural</u> is used as a <u>symbol</u> of conflict, and alludes to the apple of <u>temptation</u> and <u>sin</u> from the Bible (see page 2).

The Destruction of Sennacherib (Pages 4-5)

1) Two <u>natural similes</u> are used to describe the fate of the soldiers — at the start, the soldiers are described as <u>healthy</u> "leaves" when "<u>Summer</u> is green", but they are then likened to <u>decaying</u> leaves when "<u>Autumn</u> hath blown". This not only <u>contrasts</u> the states of <u>life</u> and <u>death</u>, but also suggests that their defeat is as natural as the seasons turning.
2) The simile "<u>melted like snow</u>" shows how <u>quickly</u> the might of Sennacherib's army is <u>destroyed</u>. The peaceful <u>natural imagery</u> suggests that their deaths were not violent, but <u>swift</u> and <u>gentle</u>.

Sometimes nature is the source of conflict

Extract from 'The Prelude' (Pages 6-7)

1) The almost <u>magical beauty</u> of nature is present in the extract, with the "<u>circles glittering</u>" on the lake and the "<u>sparkling light</u>". The speaker initially seems to be <u>inspired</u> and <u>relaxed</u> by nature.
2) However, when a <u>mountain</u> appears, it is <u>personified</u> as a <u>terrifying</u>, <u>monstrous</u> being — it "<u>Upreared</u> its head" and the speaker thinks that it "<u>Strode</u> after" him. It seems to be this that makes him <u>return</u> the boat he stole, suggesting that nature is able to <u>influence our behaviour</u>.
3) The extract ends with the phrase "a <u>trouble</u> to my <u>dreams</u>." This acts as a reminder of how nature is not just beautiful and gentle — the speaker has been <u>unsettled</u> and <u>changed</u> by the experience, and the "<u>pleasant images</u>" of nature in his mind have been <u>replaced</u> with troubling ones.

Exposure (Pages 14-15)

1) Nature is <u>personified</u> as the <u>deadly enemy</u> of the soldiers in the trenches — it has "<u>merciless</u> iced east winds that <u>knive</u>" them, and snowflakes that "come <u>feeling</u>" for their faces with "<u>fingering stealth</u>". The men don't expect to <u>die</u> from German gunfire, but from <u>exposure</u> to the <u>elements</u>.
2) There's no <u>progression</u> in the poem, which mirrors the <u>relentlessness</u> of nature. The repeated <u>stanza ending</u>, "But nothing happens", echoes the <u>monotonous</u> snow and rain that <u>fall</u> on the men.

OTHER POEMS

You could also write about 'What Were They Like?'...

Levertov uses natural imagery, such as "peaceful clouds" and "blossom", to create the impression of a tranquil and beautiful Vietnam. This contrasts with the horror and destruction wrought on the country.

Individual Experiences

No friends and nobody who understands what you're going through — it's just like being thirteen again...

> 1) Focusing on individual experiences allows the poet to present a <u>place</u>, <u>action</u> or <u>event</u> from a unique <u>point of view</u>.
>
> 2) Conflicts can leave those involved feeling <u>cut off</u> from the world.

Individuals can have unique experiences of conflict

Belfast Confetti (Pages 22-23)

1) The poem presents a very <u>personal response</u> to a <u>bomb incident</u> in Belfast.

2) It follows the <u>thoughts</u> of a panicked speaker who <u>struggles</u> to process events ("I was <u>trying</u> to complete a sentence in my head") and <u>get away</u> from <u>danger</u> ("Why can't I escape?").

3) The poet demonstrates how <u>unsafe</u> the conflict makes the speaker feel by showing how <u>familiar</u> things seem <u>strange</u>. The streets they know "so well" become a "labyrinth", their thoughts start "stuttering" and they are overwhelmed by <u>doubt</u> ("a fusillade of question-marks").

No Problem (Pages 28-29)

1) The speaker talks about their <u>personal experiences</u> with racism in the UK. They explain how people only thought of them as a black <u>stereotype</u> — they labelled the speaker as "athletic", and consequently <u>ignored</u> their individual <u>personality</u> and abilities.

2) They then describe how, despite the <u>prejudice</u> they have faced, they don't bear any <u>grudges</u> ("I have no chips on me shoulders") — they still consider the UK their "<u>Mother country</u>".

3) Finally, by adapting the <u>refrain</u> "<u>I</u> am not de problem" and proclaiming that "<u>Black</u> is not de problem", they link their personal experiences to those of all <u>black people</u> living in the UK.

Conflict can leave individuals feeling isolated

Extract from 'The Prelude' (Pages 6-7)

1) The speaker is <u>alone</u> in his "<u>act of stealth</u>" as he takes the boat and sets out across the lake. When the mountain <u>frightens</u> him, he describes it in <u>personal terms</u>, claiming that the mountain "<u>Strode after me</u>". This <u>personification</u> suggests that he feels nature is <u>reacting</u> to him as an individual.

2) He describes the <u>effect</u> the event has on him as "<u>solitude</u> / Or blank <u>desertion</u>", emphasising how the event has left him <u>isolated</u> and alone. His view of nature has been changed and he's left feeling <u>insignificant</u> compared with the "<u>huge and mighty forms</u>" of nature.

Cousin Kate (Pages 10-11)

1) The speaker was once <u>happy</u> with her "cottage-mates", but now feels <u>isolated</u> and <u>shunned</u> by society.

2) Her relationship with the lord has ruined her <u>reputation</u> — "the neighbours" see her as an "<u>outcast</u> thing". This contrasts with how they see Kate as "good and pure", emphasising the speaker's <u>isolation</u>.

3) <u>Animalistic language</u>, such as "howl" and "thing", highlight how the speaker is <u>separate</u> from <u>society</u>.

Other poems also focus on individual experiences...

'Poppies' considers the personal experience of a mother whose son has gone off to war. The speaker in 'The Class Game' discusses their personal reaction to people looking down on them because of their class.

Loss and Suffering

Two more cheery, uplifting themes here, but hey, it could be worse — at least this isn't chemistry...

> 1) <u>Loss</u> can be experienced on a <u>personal</u> level, or in a much <u>broader</u> way.
>
> 2) Some events are so <u>traumatic</u> that they cause <u>physical</u> and <u>emotional pain</u>.

Conflict causes loss on different scales

Poppies (Pages 26-27)

1) 'Poppies' focuses on the <u>personal loss</u> a mother feels when her son leaves to join the army.

2) The mother feels like she's completely <u>lost</u> her son when he goes off to war. She acts almost as if he has <u>died</u> — she leans against the "<u>war memorial</u>" and mentions "<u>Armistice Sunday</u>".

3) The loss she experiences is emphasised by references to <u>textures</u> and the <u>senses</u>. She <u>touches</u> "the <u>inscriptions</u>" on the war memorial and <u>listens</u> for her son's voice "on the <u>wind</u>" — this hints at her desperate desire to find some kind of <u>connection</u> with him to <u>compensate</u> for their <u>separation</u>.

What Were They Like? (Pages 30-31)

1) Levertov focuses on the loss of an <u>entire culture</u> — the poem shows the <u>complete devastation</u> caused by war by implying that Vietnam <u>no longer exists</u>.

2) This makes all of the answers in the poem slightly <u>uncertain</u>. The reader is reminded that "It is not remembered" — information has been <u>pieced together</u> after the <u>loss</u> of <u>cultural knowledge</u>.

3) The final sentence, "It is silent now." focuses on a lack of action. This emphasises the <u>sense of loss</u> and creates a moment of <u>reflection</u>.

It can also cause physical and mental suffering

Exposure (Pages 14-15)

1) The first line of the poem highlights the soldiers' <u>suffering</u> instantly. The phrases "Our brains <u>ache</u>" and "iced east winds that <u>knive us</u>" show that their pain is both <u>psychological</u> and <u>physical</u>.

2) They <u>sense</u> that they "are dying", but they are <u>powerless</u> and unable to change anything.

3) The soldiers ask "What are we doing here?", wondering whether they are <u>suffering</u> for <u>nothing</u>. This exposes the <u>futility</u> of war and even makes them <u>doubt</u> their <u>beliefs</u> ("love of God seems dying").

War Photographer (Pages 20-21)

1) The "small girl" is exposed to <u>incredible suffering</u>. Her <u>torment</u> is emphasised by the way she is "<u>staggering</u>" down a "devastated street". This <u>contrasts</u> with the expectation that children should be <u>carefree</u> — encountering a young girl in the middle of a war zone is <u>shocking</u> and <u>uncomfortable</u>.

2) Satyamurti further presents the <u>unfairness</u> conflict causes by showing how the girl is <u>forced</u> to carry a "baby's weight". It is <u>unnatural</u> for a child to be responsible for a baby, drawing attention to the fact that it is both a <u>physical</u> and <u>mental "burden"</u> she shouldn't have to bear.

Loss of life is a common theme in this cluster...

In 'The Destruction of Sennacherib', the entire Assyrian army is swiftly killed, causing large-scale losses. 'The Charge of the Light Brigade' also features many soldiers riding to their deaths to serve their country.

Fear and Anger

Fear and anger are just two of the negative emotions in these poems, but what do you expect from conflict?

1) <u>Fear</u> is often experienced in response to <u>uncontrollable</u> forces, such as <u>nature</u>.

2) <u>Anger</u> is a strong emotion that often stems from a <u>hurtful experience</u> or sense of <u>mistreatment</u>.

Fear can change how people feel and behave

Extract from 'The Prelude' (Pages 6-7)

1) The speaker's mood changes from carefree <u>confidence</u> to deep <u>fear</u> after encountering the mountain. This fear has a <u>lasting effect</u>, with the experience <u>troubling</u> his thoughts and dreams "<u>for many days</u>".

2) The mountain's solid "<u>stature</u>" and "<u>measured motion</u>" is <u>contrasted</u> with the speaker's "<u>trembling</u>" — the personified mountain is <u>calm</u> and <u>in control</u>, whereas the speaker <u>frantically</u> tries to <u>escape</u>.

War Photographer (Pages 20-21)

1) After the first bomb exploded, the little girl became <u>overcome</u> with <u>fear</u> — she let out a "dark <u>scream</u>", "dropped" the baby she held and "began to <u>run</u>".

2) The speaker says it was the girl's "Instinct" that caused her to do this, showing how fear can <u>influence behaviour</u> — it overrides our <u>thoughts</u> and <u>actions</u>.

"With the state of the art RemoteRevolution5000, I'm always in control."

Anger can be directed at individuals or society

A Poison Tree (Pages 2-3)

1) The speaker is <u>angry</u> with both their "<u>friend</u>" and their "<u>foe</u>", but how they <u>manage</u> their anger in each situation drastically affects the <u>outcome</u>. This suggests that anger can be more <u>harmful</u> when it is left <u>unchecked</u> and can be more easily <u>resolved</u> when it is <u>dealt with</u>.

2) Anger is described with <u>natural language</u>. It is "water'd" and "sunned" so it can "grow" both "day and night" and produce an "apple". This emphasises how <u>feeling anger</u> is a <u>natural emotion</u>.

Cousin Kate (Pages 10-11)

1) The speaker feels <u>angry</u> at how she's been <u>treated</u> by the lord. Sentences where the lord is the <u>active subject</u>, such as "He lured me", make him sound <u>predatory</u> and emphasise the idea that <u>he is responsible</u> for what happened to her.

2) She also <u>resents</u> Kate for having a good reputation and a <u>luxurious life</u>, while she is <u>miserable</u>. She expresses her anger by repeating that Kate is "<u>good and pure</u>", which creates a <u>mocking</u> tone.

Half-caste (Pages 12-13)

1) The speaker is <u>angry</u> that people use the term "half-caste" to describe people of <u>mixed race</u>. They <u>channel</u> this anger into an <u>argument</u> that explains why using the term is illogical and offensive.

2) <u>Confrontational language</u> and <u>repeated imperatives</u>, such as "Explain yuself", emphasise the speaker's anger. They <u>juxtapose</u> their <u>serious argument</u> with <u>humorous imagery</u> (e.g. "half of mih ear"). These contrasts are deliberately <u>ridiculous</u> to stress their <u>frustration</u> and how <u>wrong</u> the term "half-caste" is.

OTHER POEMS

Hopelessness is another negative emotion to think about...

Several poems, including 'Exposure' and the extract from 'The Prelude', present situations that seem hopeless. Think about how poets present such scenes, and the effects of losing hope on those involved.

Practice Questions

There are some exam-style questions just around the corner, but first here are some questions that you don't need to write a full essay to answer. One or two short paragraphs should be enough.

Conflict in Wartime

1) How does 'The Charge of the Light Brigade' show conflict on a large-scale?

2) What is the effect of the colloquial language in 'The Man He Killed'?

3) How does military conflict affect the speaker in 'Belfast Confetti'?

Conflict in Society

1) How is the tension between the mother and daughter conveyed in 'Catrin'?

2) What does the speaker in 'No Problem' suggest about stereotyping?

3) Give one example of how class divide is presented in 'The Class Game'.

Effects of Conflict

1) How does Byron describe the effects of war in 'The Destruction of Sennacherib'?

2) How does Tennyson create a sense of the men's heroism in 'The Charge of the Light Brigade'?

3) In 'Poppies', how does the mother's separation from her son affect her actions?

Reality of Conflict

1) How does the tone of 'Exposure' help to convey the reality of war?

2) How is the horror of war depicted in 'Belfast Confetti'?

3) In 'The Charge of the Light Brigade', how does the poet create a vivid picture of the battlefield?

Identity

1) In 'Catrin', how is the speaker's identity affected by her relationship with her daughter?

2) In 'Poppies', how is the mother affected by her son's new identity?

3) How does the speaker in 'Half-caste' show that their identity is important to them?

Practice Questions

Memory

1) Who do you think is more affected by their memories, the speaker in 'Poppies' or the speaker in 'Catrin'? Explain your answer.

2) How do the speaker's memories change in 'The Man He Killed'?

3) In 'What Were They Like?', how is the theme of memories used to show the effects of war?

Nature

1) What effect does the natural metaphor in 'A Poison Tree' have?

2) In the extract from 'The Prelude', how does the speaker's understanding of nature's power change?

3) How does the speaker present nature as powerful in 'Exposure'?

Individual Experiences

1) In 'Belfast Confetti', how does the speaker show how unsafe they felt?

2) Do you think that the speaker in 'No Problem' is presenting a completely personal experience? Explain your answer.

3) In the extract from 'The Prelude', why is it significant that the speaker is alone?

Loss and Suffering

1) How is the speaker's personal loss presented in 'Poppies'?

2) How does the poet create a sense of loss in 'What Were They Like'?

3) Find an example of suffering from one of the 'Conflict' poems and explain how it is presented.

Fear and Anger

1) How does the speaker's fear develop in the extract from 'The Prelude'?

2) How does the poet create a powerful sense of the girl's fear in 'War Photographer'?

3) Do you think the speaker in 'Cousin Kate' is angrier with Kate or the lord? Explain your answer.

Practice Questions

In the exam, you'll have to compare two poems which share a common theme, so no prizes for guessing what these questions are going to ask you to do. Don't try and do them all in one go — choose one, jot down a plan and have a crack at writing an answer. Then come back tomorrow and try another one.

Exam-style Questions

1) Explore the ways in which nature is portrayed as the enemy in the extract from 'The Prelude' and one other poem from 'Conflict'.

2) Compare the way that suffering is presented in 'Exposure' and one other poem from 'Conflict'.

3) Compare the way that poets present loss in 'The Man He Killed' and one other poem from 'Conflict'.

4) Compare the way that negative feelings are presented in 'A Poison Tree' and one other poem from 'Conflict'.

5) "There is no type of identity that is more important than class identity."

   Using this quotation as a starting point, write about the theme of identity in 'The Class Game' and one other poem from 'Conflict'.

   Remember to comment on how the poems are written.

Forms of Poetry

Form is about the rules poets follow when writing poetry. And like all good rules, they're there to be broken...

> 1) Form can be <u>rigid</u> and <u>regular</u> or <u>loose</u> and <u>irregular</u>.
>
> 2) Poets <u>choose</u> a form to create different <u>moods</u> and <u>effects</u>.

Some poems have a strict, regular form...

A Poison Tree (Pages 2-3)

1) The poem consists of four <u>quatrains</u> (four-line stanzas) and is written entirely in <u>rhyming couplets</u>.

2) The regular form and simple rhyme scheme <u>speed up the pace</u> of the poem and echo how fast <u>bad feelings</u> can <u>develop</u> into something more <u>sinister</u>. It also creates a <u>nursery rhyme</u> feel — the lines are <u>melodic</u> and pleasant sounding, which contrasts with the poem's dark conclusion.

Exposure (Pages 14-15)

1) The poem has a <u>rigid form</u>, with eight <u>similar</u> stanzas that each have four long lines and a <u>half-line</u> at the end. There's also an <u>ABBAC</u> rhyme scheme.

2) This form reflects the <u>monotonous existence</u> of the soldiers in the <u>trenches</u>. There is no hope of <u>change</u> for the soldiers, and the <u>half-lines</u> at the end of each stanza reinforce this — the <u>gaps</u> they leave emphasise the <u>lack</u> of action or hope.

...whereas others have a less rigid form

The Charge of the Light Brigade (Pages 16-17)

1) Tennyson uses an <u>irregular form</u> to reflect the <u>chaos</u> of war — it is made up of six <u>unique</u> stanzas, each with between six and twelve lines and a <u>different rhyme scheme</u>.

2) Although there's no regular rhyme scheme, <u>lots of rhyme</u> is used to <u>drive</u> the poem forwards like the <u>galloping cavalry</u>. <u>Rhyming triplets</u> like "reply", "why" and "die" create <u>momentum</u> that's then <u>broken</u> by an unrhymed line ("Death"). This mirrors the <u>stumbling</u> of the horses as they're shot at.

Belfast Confetti (Pages 22-23)

1) <u>Enjambment</u> and frequent <u>caesurae</u> reflect the speaker's <u>jarring</u>, <u>fragmented</u> and <u>confusing</u> experience.

2) The <u>two stanzas</u> have a <u>different number</u> of lines and <u>irregular line lengths</u>. This makes the poem look visually fragmented too, emphasising the sense of <u>instability</u> that the speaker feels.

Poppies (Pages 26-27)

1) There is <u>no regular rhyme</u> or <u>rhythm</u> in Weir's poem — it's written in <u>free verse</u>. The poem also features lots of <u>caesurae</u> in the middle of lines and a frequent use of enjambment.

2) The absence of a rigid form highlights the speaker's <u>inner turmoil</u> and how she is <u>lost in her thoughts</u>. Caesurae add moments of <u>silence</u>, which are often associated with <u>remembrance</u>, and signify the speaker trying to keep her <u>emotions</u> under control.

Other poems use specific forms...

'Cousin Kate' uses a ballad form where the lines alternate between having eight and six syllables. 'What Were They Like?' has a question and answer form where two ambiguous speakers are interacting.

Poetic Devices

If your teacher's told you to write about it, and it's got a fancy name, there's a good chance it's a poetic device.

1) Poets use all kinds of <u>devices</u> to <u>liven up</u> their writing. These pages pick out a few of the important ones, but there are <u>lots more</u> you could write about.

2) You need to be able to <u>identify</u> different techniques used in the poems and make <u>comparisons</u> between them.

3) It's really important that you don't just <u>say</u> what the technique is, but <u>comment</u> on the <u>effect</u> that it has on the poem.

Punctuation affects how a poem flows

Half-caste (Pages 12-13)

1) <u>Slashes</u> are used where the reader would normally expect question marks. This increases the <u>urgency</u> of the speaker's message by <u>speeding up</u> the pace of the poem, and makes it seem more powerful.

2) <u>Enjambment</u> reflects the speaker's <u>anger</u> as they address the reader — there is <u>no pausing</u> for breath.

3) The <u>lack of a full stop</u> at the end of the poem emphasises how this is only "<u>half</u>" of the speaker's story. It highlights how using the phrase "half-caste" means you're not seeing the <u>whole picture</u>.

Catrin (Pages 18-19)

1) <u>Enjambment</u> emphasises the <u>natural way</u> the speaker relives her memories as they surface in her mind — they <u>flow</u> into one another, rather than being <u>separate</u>.

2) However, <u>caesurae</u> and <u>end-stopping</u> at the end of the first stanza ("We want, we shouted, / To be two, to be ourselves.") <u>slow the pace</u> of the poem and emphasise the struggle to give birth. They also imitate <u>heavy breathing</u> during labour — <u>short bursts</u> of speech are followed by pauses, which mimic intakes of breath.

Repetition reinforces a point

The Charge of The Light Brigade (Pages 16-17)

1) There are <u>repeated references</u> to the "<u>six hundred</u>" men who made up the Light Brigade — repetition of the <u>number</u> emphasises the <u>human cost</u> of the battle.

2) Tennyson also uses repetition to develop a <u>vivid picture</u> of the battlefield. The repetition of phrases such as "<u>valley of Death</u>" and "<u>mouth of Hell</u>" creates a horrific, frightening scene.

3) In the third and fifth stanzas, repetition of the phrase "<u>Cannon</u> to right of them, / <u>Cannon</u> to left of them" emphasises how the Light Brigade are completely <u>surrounded</u> by Russian gunfire.

The Class Game (Pages 24-25)

1) The <u>first-</u> and <u>second-person pronouns</u> "<u>I</u>" and "<u>you</u>" are <u>repeated</u> throughout the poem. This reinforces the <u>divide</u> between the two <u>social classes</u> that the speaker discusses.

2) The <u>repeated question</u> "How can you tell what class I'm from?" highlights the speaker's <u>anger</u> at being <u>judged</u> — it bothers them so much that they can't leave it unaddressed.

3) While these questions are <u>rhetorical</u> and perhaps don't require a response, they automatically make the reader <u>think</u>, encouraging them to <u>engage</u> with the poem's <u>social issues</u>.

Poetic Devices

Poets appeal to the senses to create a vivid picture

The Destruction of Sennacherib (Pages 4-5)

1) Byron uses the sense of <u>sight</u> ("<u>gleaming</u> in <u>purple</u> and <u>gold</u>"), <u>hearing</u> ("trumpet <u>unblown</u>") and <u>touch</u> ("<u>cold</u> as the spray") to create a vivid sense of what happens to the Assyrian army.

2) This sensory imagery is used to <u>highlight</u> the <u>change</u> from <u>glory</u> (the "sheen of their spears" are "stars") to <u>defeat</u> (the soldier has "rust on his mail").

3) Likewise, the "<u>silent</u>" tents contrast with the loud "<u>wail</u>" of the widows. This appeal to the sense of hearing <u>emphasises</u> the <u>loss</u> on the battlefield.

Nick enjoyed swapping his sleigh for the spray during the off-season.

Poppies (Pages 26-27)

1) The mother's memories of her son are very <u>physical</u> (e.g. "<u>graze</u> my nose" and "playground <u>voice</u>").

2) She <u>touched</u> her son's <u>collar</u> and removed "cat hairs" from his blazer, but <u>refrained</u> from stroking his hair — their <u>physical connection</u> has <u>lessened</u> as he's grown up, and now he's physically <u>left</u> her.

3) In the final stanza, the mother says she <u>leant against</u> the war memorial and "<u>traced</u> / the inscriptions" on it — she needed to <u>physically touch</u> something to feel <u>connected</u> to her son.

Juxtaposition draws attention to similarities and differences

Cousin Kate (Pages 10-11)

1) Rossetti <u>contrasts</u> the speaker and Kate throughout the poem to highlight their <u>different circumstances</u>.

2) For example, the mirroring in "I sit and <u>howl</u> in <u>dust</u> / You sit in <u>gold</u> and <u>sing</u>" reveals the difference in their <u>wealth</u> and <u>emotional state</u>. The speaker appears poor and tormented in comparison to Kate.

War Photographer (Pages 20-21)

1) <u>Juxtaposing</u> the <u>luxury</u> of "Ascot" with the sight of "some devastated street" in a <u>war zone</u> encourages a <u>direct comparison</u> between the two locations. Introducing both scenes with "– as" invites the reader to approach them in the same way and emphasises the huge <u>differences</u> between them.

2) Likening two <u>polar opposites</u> in the phrase "<u>hell</u>, like <u>heaven</u>, is untidy" encourages the reader to consider how closely connected the two scenes in the poem might be too.

What Were They Like? (Pages 30-31)

1) Levertov <u>repeats language</u> in different contexts to create a striking contrast between <u>beautiful imagery</u> and the <u>horrific effects</u> of war. For example, in the first stanza, "<u>bone</u>" is used for "<u>ornament</u>", but in the second stanza it refers to the "<u>charred</u>" bones of the dead.

2) Presenting the violence <u>after</u> scenes of <u>tranquillity</u> makes it more shocking and draws attention to the tragic <u>change</u> from <u>peace</u> to <u>war</u>.

3) If they read each <u>question</u> and <u>answer</u> in turn, the reader will find these ideas juxtaposed even more clearly — this emphasises their effect and poignancy.

OTHER POEMS

You could also think about the use of irony...

Hardy uses irony to emphasise his message in 'The Man He Killed' — it is bitterly ironic that the speaker would almost certainly have befriended the soldier he shot under different circumstances.

Use of Sound

Poems often need to be read aloud, so the sounds words make are particularly important.

> 1) Onomatopoeia is an effective way of adding dramatic sounds to a poem.
>
> 2) Poets repeat similar sounds to create a particular mood or effect, e.g. sibilant sounds create a hissing noise which can be threatening or unsettling.

Onomatopoeia can mimic the noise of a battlefield

Exposure (Pages 14-15)

1) The onomatopoeia in "the flickering gunnery rumbles" replicates the sound of distant explosions and the shaking ground. This creates an unsettled mood, highlighting how on edge the soldiers feel.

2) The final stanza reveals how frozen the soldiers feel, both in terms of temperature and position. The onomatopoeic verbs "Shrivelling" and "puckering" emphasise the soldier's physical distortion and pain, and "crisp" mimics the harshness of the frost cracking across their faces.

The Charge of the Light Brigade (Pages 16-17)

1) Onomatopoeic verbs like "thunder'd" and "Shatter'd" imitate the chaotic, deafening noise of battle.

2) By replicating the powerful, threatening noise of the battlefield, Tennyson shows how frightening it must have been, and emphasises the heroism of the Light Brigade.

Repeated sounds create different effects

Extract from 'The Prelude' (Pages 6-7)

1) The repetition of sibilant sounds in lines 24-29 (e.g. "struck", "still", "stars") emphasises the sinister way that the mountain seems to glide after the speaker. This creates a threatening mood that reflects his fear.

2) Repetition of gentle 'l' sounds (e.g. "Small", "still", "melted all") creates consonance in lines 8-11. This produces a flowing effect, which reflects the gentle movement of the boat across the lake.

Belfast Confetti (Pages 22-23)

1) The consonance of hard 'k' sounds (e.g. "car-keys", "broken", "Makrolon") throughout the poem reinforces the destruction that's described — it mimics a cracking noise, representing the breaking of peace and order after the explosion.

2) The assonance in line 5 ("blocked with stops and / colons.") creates a repetitive 'o' sound that reflects the speaker repeatedly running into dead ends as they try to flee.

No Problem (Pages 28-29)

1) The repetition of plosive 'b' sounds ("But I bear de brunt") mimics the sound of physical blows landing. This emphasises how much the racist taunts hurt the speaker — it's like real, physical pain.

2) The sibilant 's' sounds in lines 3 and 4 ("silly playground taunts / An racist stunts") create a malicious hissing sound which reinforces the oppressive atmosphere the speaker describes.

Alliteration is another poetic use of sound...

Levertov uses alliteration ("buds ... bitter to the burned mouth") to suggest suppressed anger about war. In 'Poppies', the alliterative "hoping to hear" emphasises the mother's longing for her son's safe return.

Imagery

Imagery is when poets use language to create a picture — it includes similes, metaphors and personification.

> 1) <u>Personification</u> can make things seem more <u>real</u> or <u>lifelike</u>.
> 2) <u>Similes</u> and <u>metaphors</u> create <u>powerful descriptions</u>.

Personification gives a vivid impression of an object or place

Extract from 'The Prelude' (Pages 6-7)

1) The personification of the <u>mountain</u> makes it seem <u>threatening</u> — the phrase "<u>Upreared</u> its head" creates a <u>monstrous</u> image.

2) The personified mountain "<u>Strode after</u>" the speaker, giving a <u>vivid</u> sense that it means to <u>harm</u> him. Its calm but relentless <u>pursuit</u> increases his <u>terror</u>.

Exposure (Pages 14-15)

1) <u>Nature</u> is personified as an <u>enemy</u> of the soldiers — its "mad gusts" are described as "tugging on the wire", making the soldier's <u>surroundings</u> seem more <u>hostile</u>.

2) Dawn is <u>personified</u> as an army general — morning weather becomes "her melancholy army" which "Attacks" them. This emphasises how it seems as though the whole world is <u>against</u> the soldiers.

3) Even the usually gentle image of "Pale" snowflakes is made <u>sinister</u> through personification. They go "feeling" for the men's faces with "fingering stealth", like they are searching for <u>weaknesses</u>.

Similes and metaphors can be powerful ways of making a point

A Poison Tree (Pages 2-3)

1) Blake uses an extended metaphor throughout the poem to show how the speaker's <u>anger</u> grows over time. This is <u>represented</u> in the growth of the "tree" that produces a poisonous "apple bright".

2) Presenting a <u>feeling</u> as a <u>physical object</u> gives the reader a stronger sense of its <u>power</u>. It also makes the <u>consequences</u> of anger seem <u>greater</u>, which highlights the <u>moral message</u>.

Cousin Kate (Pages 10-11)

1) Similes compare the speaker to <u>decorative clothing</u> ("like a <u>golden knot</u>" and "like a <u>glove</u>") to <u>emphasise</u> how the lord didn't really care about her — he valued her <u>superficial appearance</u> more.

2) "I sit and howl in dust" evokes an image of the speaker as an animal, emphasising her sense of suffering. She feels outcast and '<u>dirty</u>', describing how society now just sees her as "an <u>unclean</u> <u>thing</u>". The <u>dehumanising language</u> of "thing" stresses how <u>worthless</u> society now considers her.

Catrin (Pages 18-19)

1) The "Red rope of love" is a metaphor for the <u>emotional bond</u> between the mother and child.

2) Although a "rope" implies the possibility of fraying, loosening or even severing, the association of "Red" with <u>blood</u> reminds the reader that the pair are <u>family</u> and <u>care deeply</u> about each other.

Other poems also use personification...

Both 'The Destruction of Sennacherib' and 'The Charge of the Light Brigade' personify death by giving it human attributes like "breath" and "jaws" to make it seem more real, present and threatening.

Rhyme and Rhythm

Rejoice happily, your teacher has marshmallows — there's no excuse for spelling 'rhythm' wrong in the exam.

1) Rhyme and rhythm affect the mood of a poem and how it flows.
2) They can also be used to create a particular effect or to emphasise the message of a poem.

Rhyme can reinforce a poem's message

The Destruction of Sennacherib (Pages 4-5)

1) Rhyming couplets (e.g. "fold" and "gold") drive the poem forward swiftly and steadily. This imitates the quick and relentless destruction that washes over the Assyrian army.
2) The rhymes are mostly simple and monosyllabic — they create a strong beat that gives the poem a sense of inevitability.

Exposure (Pages 14-15)

1) The regular ABBAC rhyme scheme emphasises the soldier's experience of life in the trenches. It is predictable but never quite settled — the final half-line of each stanza is always left unrhymed, which reflects the tension and unease felt by the soldiers.
2) Many of the rhymes are half-rhymes (e.g. "knive us" and "nervous"), so there isn't a sense of completion. Readers wait for a rhyme that never fully arrives, like the soldiers anxiously wait for something to happen.

A poem's rhythm affects its pace and mood

The Man He Killed (Pages 8-9)

1) The regular iambic metre (one unstressed syllable followed by one stressed one) mimics natural speech rhythms and makes the speaker seem comfortable, friendly and happy.
2) However, in the third and fourth stanzas, this rhythm is broken up by caesurae. This emphasises how the speaker begins to question himself and doubt his reasons for killing the other soldier.

The Charge of the Light Brigade (Pages 16-17)

1) The regular rhythm creates a sense of the energy and speed of the cavalry charging into battle. The sense of action and excitement also helps to emphasise the soldiers' heroism.
2) The metre is mainly dactylic — one stressed syllable is followed by two unstressed ones (e.g. "All in the valley of Death"). This creates a galloping effect, like the sound of the horses' hooves.

War Photographer (Pages 20-21)

1) The irregular rhythm reflects the idea the 'frames' can have flexibility — the rhythm isn't fixed. It also creates an honest mood — the speaker's thoughts haven't been changed to fit a set rhythm.
2) Caesurae and end-stopping, such as in line 16 ("She saw me seeing her; my finger pressed."), slow down the pace of the poem and give the reader time to contemplate what the speaker is saying. This counters the public tendency to skim over bad news and focus on the positive.

Rhyme schemes are important in other poems...

'A Poison Tree' has a regular AABB rhyme scheme which reflects the friend / foe contrast. The extract from 'The Prelude' lacks a conventional rhyme scheme to reflect how little control man has over nature.

Voice

The voice is a key feature of a poem — it can have a big effect on how the poet's message is conveyed.

> 1) A <u>first-person voice</u> gives you one person's <u>perspective</u>.
>
> 2) Poetry can reproduce <u>spoken language</u> to hint at the <u>speaker's character</u>.

Using a first-person speaker makes the poem more personal

The Man He Killed (Pages 8-9)

1) The use of <u>first-person pronouns</u>, such as "<u>I</u>", "<u>me</u>" and "<u>my</u>", show that these are an individual's very <u>personal thoughts</u> and <u>experiences</u> of war.

2) The use of <u>colloquial</u>, <u>informal language</u>, such as "wet / Right many a nipperkin!", shows that the speaker is just an ordinary individual and encourages the reader to respond <u>sympathetically</u>.

Poppies (Pages 26-27)

1) Using a first-person speaker allows Weir to express the mother's <u>memories</u> and <u>emotions</u>, e.g. "<u>I was brave</u>". The mother speaks <u>personally</u> and <u>intimately</u>, as if she is revealing her most <u>private thoughts</u>.

2) <u>Domestic</u> language and imagery gives the mother a <u>unique</u> voice. For example, she describes her <u>nervousness</u> with <u>sewing imagery</u> — "my stomach busy / <u>making tucks, darts, pleats</u>".

No Problem (Pages 28-29)

1) The speaker repeats the <u>personal pronoun</u> "I" in several <u>positive</u> phrases, e.g. "<u>I am</u> born academic" and "<u>I can</u> teach yu", which shows how they recognise their own <u>value</u>.

2) This shows the <u>strength</u> of the speaker's <u>character</u> and encourages the reader to admire them — they do not doubt their own <u>ability</u> or <u>potential</u> despite all the oppression they have faced.

Poems can include features of spoken language

The Class Game (Pages 24-25)

1) Casey uses <u>colloquial language</u> (e.g. "bum" and "bog") and Liverpudlian <u>dialect</u> (e.g. "corpy") to give the poem an <u>authentic voice</u> and make it sound like a <u>spoken account</u>.

2) This shows that, while the speaker is criticised for their voice, they are <u>proud</u> of it and won't change it. The authentic voice also makes the speaker seem <u>real</u>, which encourages the reader to <u>sympathise</u> with them.

Half-caste (Pages 12-13)

Leo's pride would never forgive him if he let the vultures pinch dinner again.

1) <u>Phonetic spellings</u> (e.g. "yuself" and "dat") reflect the speaker's <u>Caribbean accent</u> — this shows that they are <u>proud</u> of their Caribbean <u>heritage</u>.

2) The phonetic spellings also reinforce the speaker's <u>anger</u>, e.g. "wid" and "dem" are <u>more forceful</u> sounds than 'with' and 'them'.

Third-person speakers are more removed from the action...

The speakers in 'The Destruction of Sennacherib' and 'The Charge of the Light Brigade' are able to comment on the battles from afar. Describing large scenes like this makes them seem grander.

Beginnings of Poems

Poets know that first impressions are important, so there's usually something to say about openings of poems.

> 1) The <u>beginning</u> of a poem often <u>sets the tone</u> for the rest of the poem.
>
> 2) Poets aim to <u>draw in</u> their readers, and to establish something of the poem's <u>meaning</u>.

Some openings set the scene...

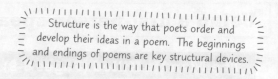

Structure is the way that poets order and develop their ideas in a poem. The beginnings and endings of poems are key structural devices.

The Man He Killed (Pages 8-9)

1) The <u>personal pronouns</u> "he" and "I" in the first stanza immediately tell the reader that the poem will focus on a personal interaction between <u>two people</u>. The use of <u>colloquial</u> and <u>friendly</u> language ("some old ancient inn") also creates a <u>positive tone</u>.

2) However, the use of "Had" and "should have" hints that the interaction actually took place in far <u>different circumstances</u>. This <u>intrigues</u> the reader, encouraging them to <u>discover</u> what <u>really happened</u>.

Cousin Kate (Pages 10-11)

1) The use of the <u>past tense</u> in the opening stanza reveals that the speaker is <u>no longer</u> a "cottage-maiden" who is "Contented" with her life. This hints that she has <u>suffered</u> through a <u>bad experience</u>.

2) The <u>questions</u> that make up lines 5 to 8 start with "Why did a great lord find me out", <u>introducing</u> the events that led to this experience. These questions create a sense of <u>despair</u>, which draws the reader in by creating a sense of <u>mystery</u> and a desire to <u>find out</u> more.

What Were They Like? (Pages 30-31)

1) The questions in the first stanza introduce a <u>sense of wonder</u> around <u>Vietnamese culture</u>. The peaceful behaviours and artistic culture that is asked about makes life sound idyllic.

2) However, the use of the <u>past tense</u> (e.g. "<u>Did they</u>") implies that none of these traditions take place any more. This hints at the <u>tragic human loss</u> which is revealed later in the poem.

...while others launch straight into the action

Half-caste (Pages 12-13)

1) The poem starts with the speaker <u>directly addressing</u> the reader ("Excuse me"). This is extended into the start of the second stanza, which begins more <u>aggressively</u> with "Explain yuself / wha yu mean". Readers are immediately <u>forced to engage</u> with the poem and <u>think</u> about their behaviour.

2) This makes the <u>reader</u> feel <u>involved</u> — they can't passively read the poem, they are <u>participating</u> in it.

Belfast Confetti (Pages 22-23)

1) The poem begins *in medias res* (in the middle of the action) — this puts the reader in a similarly <u>confused</u> position to the speaker who found himself in the <u>aftermath</u> of a bomb incident.

2) Starting the poem with the dramatic <u>adverb</u> "<u>Suddenly</u>" establishes a <u>sense of urgency</u> and reflects the sense of <u>panic</u> that is present throughout the poem. It also grabs the <u>reader's attention</u>.

OTHER POEMS

You can comment on the beginning of any poem...

'The Charge of the Light Brigade' begins with rhythmic repetition that immediately gives a sense of movement. The extract from 'The Prelude' opens with a phrase that makes it sound like a fairy tale.

Endings of Poems

Relief might be your emotion when you reach the end of a poem, but please don't write that in your exam...

> 1) Last lines can <u>sum up</u> or neatly <u>round off</u> a poem.
>
> 2) Poems often end with a <u>powerful</u> or <u>memorable</u> image.

Paul feared that the ending might not be as fun as the beginning.

Last lines can create a sense of finality...

The Charge of the Light Brigade (Pages 16-17)

1) The last stanza of the poem is the <u>shortest</u>, with only <u>six lines</u>. This can be seen to reflect the "<u>six hundred</u>" soldiers and how many of their lives were <u>cut short</u>.

2) No new concepts are introduced in this final stanza, and the <u>repetition</u> of "Honour" in lines 53 and 54 creates a sense of <u>closure</u> by <u>reinforcing</u> the commemorative message of the poem.

3) Every stanza ends with "six hundred", so the reader may expect some form of <u>conclusion</u> when this phrase appears. The last line is the only time an <u>exclamation mark</u> closes a stanza, which signals the end of the poem by expressing a more final conclusion than the previous stanzas.

The Class Game (Pages 24-25)

1) In the final section of the poem (from line 22 onwards), the speaker stops <u>comparing</u> the two classes. They proudly state the facts about who they are in short, decisive lines rather than using rhetorical questions. This shows that they have <u>accepted</u> themselves despite the opinions of others.

2) This idea is emphasised by turning the poem's <u>rhetorical question</u> ("How can you tell what class I'm from?") into a <u>statement</u> in the final line ("I'm proud of the class that I come from").

...or they can leave you with doubts

A Poison Tree (Pages 2-3)

1) The final line ("My foe outstretch'd beneath the tree.") is <u>shocking</u>, and <u>contrasts</u> with the <u>nursery-rhyme feel</u> that is established by the regular AABB rhyme scheme and simple rhythm.

2) This ending is <u>ambiguous</u>. It is <u>not clear</u> whether the "outstretch'd" foe is dead or alive, although the <u>sinister tone</u> implies a darker ending to the poem.

3) This ambiguity is increased by the phrase "In the morning glad I see". Either the <u>morning</u> or the <u>speaker</u> could be "glad" — <u>not knowing</u> for sure how the <u>speaker feels</u> prevents the reader from knowing how to feel themselves.

War Photographer (Pages 20-21)

1) The last three lines <u>unsettle</u> the reader by reminding them that even if people choose to view the world through a safe "frame", the reality of war and all its <u>brutality</u> is still out there.

2) The final image of "a blood stain on a wall" is <u>violent</u> and likely to stick in the reader's mind. The image might imply that the little girl died, which ends the poem on a note of uncertainty, especially as the reader is <u>never truly sure</u> what happened to her.

OTHER POEMS

Other poems feature interesting endings...

'No Problem' and 'Cousin Kate' end by anticipating a better future for themselves and others. In contrast, 'Exposure' and 'Belfast Confetti' both end on negative images of unresolved suffering.

Section Three — Poetic Techniques

Mood

Sadly there are no teenage-angst poems in this cluster, but there's still plenty for you to write about moods.

> 1) The mood is the <u>feeling</u> or <u>atmosphere</u> created in a poem.
> 2) Poets often <u>change</u> the mood of the poem as it progresses.

Imagery can be used to create a specific mood

The Destruction of Sennacherib (Pages 4-5)

1) <u>Natural imagery</u> creates a mood of <u>inevitability</u>. By comparing the destruction of the Assyrian army to "leaves" when "Autumn hath blown", Byron implies that it's only natural that they fall.

2) Describing the <u>horse's death</u> with imagery associated with the <u>sea</u> creates a <u>violent mood</u>. The image of the "foam of his gasping" being like the cold "spray" of the "rock-beating surf" reminds the reader of waves <u>crashing furiously</u> against rocks. This emphasises the <u>physical intensity</u> of his death.

Exposure (Pages 14-15)

1) <u>Bleak natural imagery</u> reflects the <u>hopeless</u>, <u>dejected mood</u> of the soldiers.

2) <u>Traditional poetic imagery</u> is <u>subverted</u> to emphasise the <u>grim</u> nature of their experience. "<u>Dawn</u>" brings <u>misery</u> instead of <u>hope</u>, and the <u>snow</u> is "<u>black</u>" and "<u>deathly</u>" rather than <u>white</u> and <u>pure</u>. Even the "<u>fires</u>" of home are "crusted dark-red <u>jewels</u>" — they offer <u>no warmth</u> or comfort.

3) The <u>repetition</u> of "<u>But nothing happens</u>" also contributes to the <u>tedious</u>, <u>monotonous</u> mood. It confirms that there is <u>little hope</u> of the mood <u>changing</u>.

Some poems have a change in mood

Extract from 'The Prelude' (Pages 6-7)

1) At the start of the extract, the mood is mostly <u>happy</u>, <u>light</u> and <u>carefree</u> — the speaker seems <u>confident</u> and <u>comfortable</u>, and nature seems <u>beautiful</u> and <u>tranquil</u>.

2) However, the mood <u>changes</u> suddenly with the line "When, from behind that craggy steep till then". It becomes <u>sinister</u> and <u>threatening</u> as the mountain seems to have a "purpose of its own", pursuing the speaker with "measured motion" — <u>personification</u> emphasises the mountain's <u>power</u> and <u>hostility</u>.

3) The extract ends in a <u>philosophical mood</u> — the speaker <u>reflects</u> on the <u>experience</u> and his new <u>understanding</u> of nature's <u>power</u>.

What Were They Like? (Pages 30-31)

1) The mood in the first stanza is <u>gentle</u> and <u>peaceful</u> as the speaker asks about "the opening of buds" and "quiet laughter" that may have existed in Vietnam. However, the use of the <u>past tense</u> also hints at a <u>sense of loss</u>.

2) In the second stanza, there's a shift to a more <u>sombre</u>, <u>mournful</u> mood. This shift in mood is emphasised by the <u>question and answer form</u>, which creates more direct <u>comparisons</u> between the <u>past</u> (e.g. the "<u>lanterns</u> of stone") and the <u>present</u> (e.g. how "<u>hearts</u> turned to stone").

'Catrin' and 'No Problem' also have shifts in mood...

OTHER POEMS

The sense of monotony before the birth in 'Catrin' drastically changes once the speaker's struggle begins. In 'No Problem', the speaker becomes more hopeful when thinking about the future instead of their past.

Practice Questions

It's the end of another section, so you know what that means — handy questions to see how well you've absorbed everything you've just read. Try to answer them without looking back through the section.

Forms of Poetry

1) Explain how the form of 'Exposure' mirrors the experience of the soldiers.

2) Comment on the form of 'The Charge of the Light Brigade'. How does it reflect the chaos of war?

3) In 'Poppies', how does Weir use form to convey the internal struggle of the speaker?

Poetic Devices

1) Give an example of enjambment in 'Half-caste' and explain its effect.

2) Give an example of caesurae in 'Catrin'. What effect does it have?

3) How does Casey use repetition in 'The Class Game'? What does it suggest about the speaker?

4) How does Byron appeal to the reader's senses in 'The Destruction of Sennacherib'?

5) In 'Cousin Kate', how does Rossetti use juxtaposition to show the divide between the two women?

6) How do contrasts in 'What Were They Like?' make the loss of Vietnam more touching?

Use of Sound

1) Do you think that the sounds of the battlefield are more realistic in 'Exposure' or 'The Charge of the Light Brigade'? Explain your answer.

2) Give some examples of repeated sounds in 'Belfast Confetti'. What effect do they have?

3) Give some examples of plosive words in 'No Problem' and explain their effect.

Imagery

1) In the extract from 'The Prelude', how does Wordsworth use personification to make the speaker's encounter seem more frightening?

2) Explain the meaning and significance of the extended metaphor in 'A Poison Tree'.

3) In 'Cousin Kate', how are similes used to show the speaker's feeling of abandonment?

Practice Questions

Rhyme and Rhythm

1) Describe the effect of the rhyming couplets in 'The Destruction of Sennacherib'.

2) Explain how Owen uses rhyme in 'Exposure' to emphasise the way that the soldiers feel.

3) How does the rhythm of 'War Photographer' contribute to the mood of the poem?

Voice

1) How does the first-person voice help the reader sympathise with the speaker in 'The Man He Killed'?

2) In 'No Problem', how does Zephaniah encourage the reader to admire the speaker?

3) What is the effect of the colloquial language in 'The Class Game'?

Beginnings of Poems

1) How does the beginning of 'Cousin Kate' set the scene for the rest of the poem?

2) Why do you think Agard chose to start 'Half-caste' by directly addressing the reader?

3) Choose a poem not mentioned on page 56 and write about the effect of its opening.

Endings of Poems

1) How does the ending of 'The Charge of the Light Brigade' reinforce the poem's main message?

2) Why do you think the speaker in 'The Class Game' stops asking questions at the end of the poem?

3) What is the effect of the last two lines of 'A Poison Tree'?

Mood

1) What is the mood in the first stanza of 'Exposure'? Is this mood consistent throughout the poem?

2) What is the mood at the end of the extract from 'The Prelude'? How is this mood created?

3) In 'What Were They Like?', what is the effect of the shift in mood?

Practice Questions

Here's your third and final batch of exam-style questions. Sections Four and Five have lots of handy advice about writing a great exam answer, so have a read of those pages if you're looking for some hints and tips.

Exam-style Questions

1) Compare the ways in which individual experiences are portrayed in 'Catrin' and one other poem from 'Conflict'.

2) Compare the ways that poets present the effects of conflict in 'What Were They Like?' and one other poem from 'Conflict'.

3) "A first-person speaker is the most effective way of conveying human emotions in a poem."

   Using this statement as a starting point, compare the use of voice in 'No Problem' and one other poem from 'Conflict'.

4) Compare the ways conflict on the battlefield is presented in 'The Charge of The Light Brigade' and one other poem from 'Conflict'.

5) Compare the ways that poets present negative emotions in 'Cousin Kate' and one other poem from 'Conflict'.

The Poetry Exam

For your Edexcel English Literature course, you'll have to sit two exams — Paper 1 and Paper 2. This book will help you prepare for the Poetry Anthology section, which is part of Paper 2.

This is how your Paper 2 exam will work

1) The Paper 2 exam lasts for 2 hours and 15 minutes. It will be split into three parts, like this:

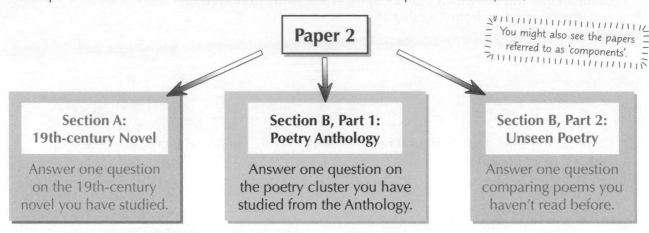

Paper 2

You might also see the papers referred to as 'components'.

Section A:
19th-century Novel

Answer one question on the 19th-century novel you have studied.

Section B, Part 1:
Poetry Anthology

Answer one question on the poetry cluster you have studied from the Anthology.

Section B, Part 2:
Unseen Poetry

Answer one question comparing poems you haven't read before.

2) The next few pages give you tips on how to answer the question in Section B, Part 1.

3) Section B, Part 1 has one question about each poetry cluster. You should only answer one of these questions — make sure you answer the question on the 'Conflict' cluster.

4) Section B, Part 1 is worth 20 marks, which is about 12.5% of your entire GCSE. In the exam, you should spend about 35 minutes on Section B, Part 1.

5) You're not allowed to take your own anthology or any notes about the poems into the exam.

Read the question carefully and underline key words

1) Read the question for 'Conflict' carefully. Underline the theme and any other key words.

2) The question will give you one poem and ask you to compare it with any other poem from the same cluster. You'll be given a list of all the poems to help you choose — pick one that relates to the theme.

3) Here's the kind of question you'll get in the exam:

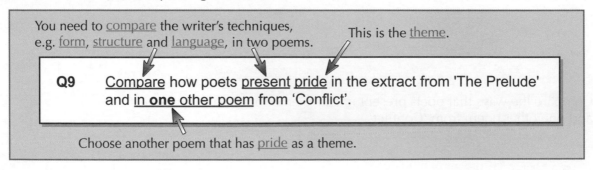

You need to compare the writer's techniques, e.g. form, structure and language, in two poems.   This is the theme.

Q9   Compare how poets present pride in the extract from 'The Prelude' and in **one** other poem from 'Conflict'.

Choose another poem that has pride as a theme.

There are three main ways to get marks

There are three main things to keep in mind when you're planning and writing your answer:

- Give your own thoughts and opinions on the poems and support them with quotes from the text.
- Explain the effects of features like form, structure and language.
- Describe the similarities and differences between poems and their contexts.

How to Structure Your Answer

A solid structure is essential — it lets the examiner follow your argument nice and easily. The best way to make sure you write a well-structured essay in the exam is to make a plan before you start writing (see p.67).

Start with an introduction and end with a conclusion

1) Your introduction should begin by giving a clear answer to the question in a sentence or two. Use the rest of the introduction to briefly develop this idea — try to include some of the main ideas from your plan.

2) The main body of your essay should be three to five paragraphs that compare the two poems.

3) Finish your essay with a conclusion — this should summarise your answer to the question. It's also your last chance to impress the examiner, so try to make your final sentence memorable.

Compare the poems throughout your essay

1) In each paragraph of the main body, write about one poem and then explain whether the other poem is similar or different. Don't just write several paragraphs about one poem, followed by several paragraphs about the other.

2) Every paragraph should compare a feature of the poems, such as their form, their structure, the language they use or the feelings they put across.

Remember to start a new paragraph every time you start comparing a new feature of the poems.

3) Link your ideas with words like 'similarly', 'likewise' or 'equally' when you're writing about a similarity. Or use phrases such as 'in contrast' and 'on the other hand' if you're explaining a difference.

Use P.E.E.D. to structure each paragraph

1) P.E.E.D. stands for: Point, Example, Explain, Develop.

> **POINT** — Begin each paragraph by making a comparison between the two poems.
>
> **EXAMPLE** — Then give an example from one of the poems.
>
> **EXPLAIN** — Explain how the example supports your opening point.
>
> **DEVELOP** — Develop your point by writing about its effect on the reader, how it links to another part of the poem, how it relates to the poem's context, or by adding to the comparison with the other poem.

After you've explained your first example, give an example from the other poem and explain that too.

2) This is just a framework to make sure your paragraphs have all the features they need to pick up marks — you don't have to follow it rigidly in every paragraph.

3) Here's an example of how you could use P.E.E.D. to structure a paragraph:

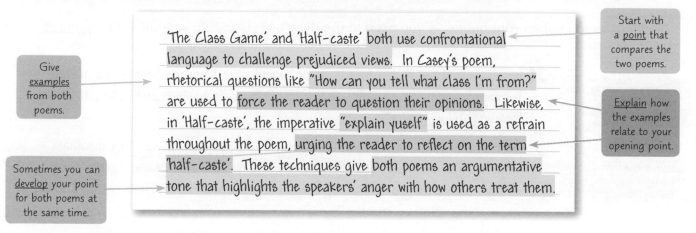

Give examples from both poems.

'The Class Game' and 'Half-caste' both use confrontational language to challenge prejudiced views. In Casey's poem, rhetorical questions like "How can you tell what class I'm from?" are used to force the reader to question their opinions. Likewise, in 'Half-caste', the imperative "explain yuself" is used as a refrain throughout the poem, urging the reader to reflect on the term 'half-caste'. These techniques give both poems an argumentative tone that highlights the speakers' anger with how others treat them.

Start with a point that compares the two poems.

Explain how the examples relate to your opening point.

Sometimes you can develop your point for both poems at the same time.

Index

Answers

These are the answers to the exercises in Section Five. They're only suggestions, so don't worry if what you've written doesn't match exactly — there are lots of possible answers.

Page 70 — Adding Quotes and Developing Points

Sample Plan

    (A) "an apple bright"

    (B) "soft deceitful wiles"

    (C) "of course he was; / That's clear enough; although"

    (D) "Right many a nipperkin!"

    (E) The nursery rhyme feel of the poem emphasises its moral message, making the reader think about their own feelings of anger.

    (F) The detached language which describes the shooting makes the reader consider if soldiers really believe in the things they are fighting for.

Answer Extract 1

    (A) "I sit and howl in dust"

    (B) "an unclean thing"

    (C) "All the bones were charred"

Answer Extract 2

    (A) "good and pure"

    (B) "peaceful clouds"

    (C) "It is not remembered"

Page 71 — Adding Quotes and Developing Points

Answer Extract 1

    (A) This highlights how it's not only her social standing and wealth that have been affected, but also things that are vital to her emotional and personal identity, such as her "heart".

    (B) Using speakers who are more distanced from the loss emphasises this idea, as unlike the speaker in 'Cousin Kate', they can piece together the scale of the loss from what was "reported".

Answer Extract 2

    (A) The repeated questioning and hypothetical phrases indicate that the speaker's loss has been so great that she can't move on with her life.

    (B) Unlike the speaker in 'Cousin Kate', who is unable to move on from the past, the scale of the loss in Levertov's poem means that the speakers are actively trying to reconstruct the past.

Answer Extract 3

    (A) The rhyme scheme also hints at the loneliness of the speaker — couplets would signal a sense of completeness, but the lack of regularity reflects how she's been abandoned.

    (B) This irregular form also mirrors the lack of order that would be found in a world which has allowed an entire nation to be destroyed.

Page 73 — Marking Answer Extracts

Answer Extract 1

    I think this answer would get a grade 4-5 because it makes a point that compares the two poems and supports the point with quotes from the poems. To get a higher grade, it needs to develop the ideas more fully and explain the effect of the quotes in more detail.

Answer Extract 2

    I think this answer would get a grade 8-9 because it gives a detailed analysis of the poets' use of language, uses the correct technical vocabulary and offers different interpretations of the phrases "branded" and "label".

Answer Extract 3

    I think this answer is a grade 6-7. It makes a good point to compare the poems, and it suggests what the impact on the reader might be. For a higher grade, the effect of the quotes could be explained in more detail.

Page 74 — Marking Answer Extracts

Answer Extract 1

    I think this answer would get a grade 8-9 because it integrates examples from the poems and explains them effectively. It also includes relevant knowledge of context.

Answer Extract 2

    I think this answer would get a grade 4-5 because it makes points about the poems and backs them up with examples. For a higher grade, it needs more explanation of how the quotes support the points and how they affect the reader.

Answer Extract 3

    I would give this extract a grade 6-7 because it makes a point, gives examples from the text, starts to develop points and uses some relevant context. To get a higher grade, more in-depth analysis of techniques is needed.

Pages 75-76 — Marking a Whole Answer

    I think this answer should be awarded a grade 8-9 because it makes a wide range of detailed comparisons and focuses on the effects of form, language and symbolism on the reader. It also makes relevant reference to context, uses a range of technical vocabulary, and gives well-explained examples of the poets' techniques.

ACEHR41